Ellen
DeGeneres

Ellen DeGeneres

by Katie Sharp

LUCENT BOOKS
A part of Gale, Cengage Learning

Detroit • New York • San Francisco • New Haven, Conn • Waterville, Maine • London

Ellen DeGeneres

45366

GALE
CENGAGE Learning·

LIBRARY OF CONGRESS CATALOGING-IN-PUBLICATION DATA

Sharp, Katie John.
  Ellen DeGeneres / by Katie Sharp.
    p. cm. -- (People in the news)
  Includes bibliographical references and index.
  ISBN 978-1-4205-0234-3 (hardcover)
  1. DeGeneres, Ellen--Juvenile literature. 2. Comedians--United States--Biography--Juvenile literature. 3. Television personalities--United States--Biography--Juvenile literature. I. Title.
  PN2287.D358S53 2010
  792.702'8092--dc22
  [B]
                                                          2009032214

Lucent Books
27500 Drake Rd.
Farmington Hills, MI 48331

ISBN-13: 978-1-4205-0234-3
ISBN-10: 1-4205-0234-4

Printed in the United States of America
1 2 3 4 5 6 7 13 12 11 10 09

Printed by Bang Printing, Brainerd, MN, 1ˢᵗ Ptg., 12/2009

Contents

Fame and celebrity are alluring. People are drawn to those who walk in fame's spotlight, whether they are known for great accomplishments or for notorious deeds. The lives of the famous pique public interest and attract attention, perhaps because their experiences seem in some ways so different from, yet in other ways so similar to, our own.

Newspapers, magazines, and television regularly capitalize on this fascination with celebrity by running profiles of famous people. For example, television programs such as *Entertainment Tonight* devote all of their programming to stories about entertainment and entertainers. Magazines such as *People* fill their pages with stories of the private lives of famous people. Even newspapers, newsmagazines, and television news frequently delve into the lives of well-known personalities. Despite the number of articles and programs, few provide more than a superficial glimpse at their subjects.

Lucent's People in the News series offers young readers a deeper look into the lives of today's newsmakers, the influences that have shaped them, and the impact they have had in their fields of endeavor and on other people's lives. The subjects of the series hail from many disciplines and walks of life. They include authors, musicians, athletes, political leaders, entertainers, entrepreneurs, and others who have made a mark on modern life and who, in many cases, will continue to do so for years to come.

These biographies are more than factual chronicles. Each book emphasizes the contributions, accomplishments, or deeds that have brought fame or notoriety to the individual and shows how that person has influenced modern life. Authors portray their subjects in a realistic, unsentimental light. For example, Bill Gates—the cofounder and chief executive officer of the software giant Microsoft—has been instrumental in making personal computers the most vital tool of the modern age. Few dispute his business savvy, his perseverance, or his technical expertise, yet critics say he is ruthless in his dealings with competitors and driven more by his desire to maintain Microsoft's dominance in the computer industry than by an interest in furthering technology.

In these books, young readers will encounter inspiring stories about real people who achieved success despite enormous obstacles. Oprah Winfrey—the most powerful, most watched, and wealthiest woman on television today—spent the first six years of her life in the care of her grandparents while her unwed mother sought work and a better life elsewhere. Her adolescence was colored by promiscuity, pregnancy at age fourteen, rape, and sexual abuse.

Each author documents and supports his or her work with an array of primary and secondary source quotations taken from diaries, letters, speeches, and interviews. All quotes are footnoted to show readers exactly how and where biographers derive their information and provide guidance for further research. The quotations enliven the text by giving readers eyewitness views of the life and accomplishments of each person covered in the People in the News series.

In addition, each book in the series includes photographs, annotated bibliographies, timelines, and comprehensive indexes. For both the casual reader and the student researcher, the People in the News series offers insight into the lives of today's newsmakers—people who shape the way we live, work, and play in the modern age.

Lessons in Perseverance

With twenty-five daytime Emmys, Ellen DeGeneres has created one of the most popular and successful daytime talk shows to hit the small screen. Her guests include Hollywood's hottest celebrities, chart-topping musical talent, everyday people who have done extraordinary things, and adoring fans plucked from the audience to participate in wacky contests or dance onstage.

But viewers do not tune in to *The Ellen DeGeneres Show* every weekday just to see who is sitting in the chair next to the blonde-haired, blue-eyed comedian/talk-show host. They want to watch and listen to DeGeneres herself. They want to see her make a fool of herself as she dances to tunes spun by her DJ, Tony. They want to laugh as she uses her dry wit to make fun of everyday situations. They want to witness what special gesture this kind, giving person, who seemingly has it all, will extend to some person, animal, or charity in need.

Just over ten years ago, such success seemed impossible for this stand-up comic from New Orleans. At what seemed to be the height of her career, in 1997, with a successful stand-up career, a hit television series, and a best-selling book, DeGeneres decided to come out of the closet and announce publicly that she is gay. Although many had already assumed that she was, she wanted to set the record straight, to address the rumors and gossip. DeGeneres timed her announcement so that she and her character, Ellen Morgan, whom she played on her television show *Ellen*, would come out at about the same time. What DeGeneres wanted to do would make television history: Ellen Morgan would be the first gay female lead in a television series.

Although many colleagues and friends questioned DeGeneres's motives, the comedian knew exactly what she was doing. She wanted to be true to herself. She did not want to hide who she was anymore. Many people, including those in the gay and lesbian community, applauded her move; others, including some high-profile religious leaders and the show's sponsors, were not happy and condemned her decision. Many others were somewhere in the middle; they did not care that DeGeneres was gay—in fact, they assumed she was—they simply did not think it was necessary for her to be so open about her sexuality. They just wanted to laugh at her comedy without knowing the details of her life.

But Ellen DeGeneres had made up her mind, and she convinced the executives and producers at ABC/Disney to go along with her. In an episode code-named "The Puppy Episode"—to keep its subject matter a closely guarded secret—and written in part by DeGeneres herself, Ellen Morgan revealed to her friends that she was gay. At the same time, Ellen DeGeneres appeared on the cover of *Time* magazine with the quip, "Yep, I'm Gay."

The episode in which Ellen Morgan revealed her sexuality was well received by both viewers and critics. They felt the subject matter was well handled—and it was funny. In the following year, DeGeneres garnered two Emmy nominations—one for her performance in that episode, and the other for her role in writing the script. With much joy and pride, she accepted the writing award. But although the show was doing well, *Ellen* lasted only one more season. It was canceled in 1998. Soon after, DeGeneres went through a very public breakup with her actress girlfriend, Anne Heche.

After revealing her homosexuality, DeGeneres felt that her fans and the entertainment industry had turned on her. She was certain nobody liked her anymore. She began to get fewer offers for work. But instead of hiding out and feeling sorry for herself, she went back to doing what she does best: stand-up comedy.

As a child, Ellen DeGeneres did not aspire to make people laugh—she just did it naturally. With her family making constant

Ellen and her companion Anne Heche (right) applaud Bill Clinton at a Human Rights Campaign Fund dinner in 1997. It was the first time a president had spoken at a gay and lesbian event.

moves around the New Orleans area, DeGeneres found herself having to start over in a new school and make new friends time after time. She used her gift of humor to make the people around her notice her; she made friends by making people laugh.

DeGeneres also used humor to get her mother through some tough times. When DeGeneres was thirteen her parents separated, and she took it upon herself to make her mother, Betty, see the humor in the situation. And when Betty was diagnosed with breast cancer, Ellen never left her side.

So when the time came for Ellen DeGeneres to pick herself up and get her career on the right track again, she wrote a comedy routine appropriately called *The Beginning* and took it on the road. She filmed the show for HBO, and audiences loved it. But what really turned her career around was her ability to make Americans laugh again following the 2001 terrorist attacks. Hosting the Emmy Awards just two months after the tragedy, she received rave reviews and a standing ovation for her delicate handling of the show. And since that time, DeGeneres has found herself working steadily as her career rebounded.

Soon after hosting the 2001 Emmy Awards show, DeGeneres found herself much in demand. She lent her voice to a fish named Dory in the film *Finding Nemo,* did another HBO comedy special, and started what would become her award-winning talk show. She also has helped the citizens of her native New Orleans in the aftermath of Hurricane Katrina; started a pet food company; married the love of her life, Portia de Rossi; became a spokesmodel for CoverGirl; and plans to appear in another motion picture. And in August 2009 DeGeneres agreed to serve as the fourth judge on the popular TV show *American Idol.*

With all the ups and downs in her life, Ellen DeGeneres has shown everyone around her and who watches her what it takes to persevere in show business and in life—laughter.

Chapter 1

Growing Up Ellen

Ellen DeGeneres opens her 1995 best-selling book *My Point . . . and I Do Have One* with several questions: "Who am I? How did I get to be me? If I wasn't me, who would I be?"[1] And that is indeed a good place to begin to explore and understand this blonde-haired, blue-eyed comedian who has faced so many ups and downs in both her personal and professional lives, but who continues to make jokes and keep everyone around her laughing.

A Comedian Is Born

DeGeneres goes on to answer her own questions, weaving in a bit of humor as only she can: "I was born in Metairie, Louisiana, at Ocsnar Hospital, January 26, 1958. I lived in a house on Haring Road in Metairie until I was . . . oh, let's say eight or nine—maybe ten . . . could've been seven or six. I don't know."[2]

Metairie is an incorporated area next to the city of New Orleans. DeGeneres's parents, Elliott and Elizabeth "Betty," already had a four-year-old son, Vance, when Ellen was born. In her 1999 book, *Love, Ellen: A Mother/Daughter Journey*, Betty DeGeneres writes of having to convince her husband to have another child: "Ellen was indeed a miracle. I had to beg for a second child. Elliott thought one child, whom we dearly loved, was sufficient. Nothing if not tenacious, I didn't give up. I thank God every day that I persevered, and so does Elliott."[3]

Elliott was an insurance salesman; Betty worked as an administrative assistant while also taking care of their two children. Both were devoted Christian Scientists, which is how they met, and they raised their children with the faith as well. According to Betty, the family relied on prayer as its guide. And as Christian Scientists, her children never received vaccinations or medications of any kind and attended Sunday school to learn about the Bible and prayer. Betty believed that giving her children a strong spiritual foundation was a good, important thing—that all children need to know that, like their parents, God loves them just the way they are, no matter what.

Ellen's mother, Betty, shown in 2004, was an administrative assistant while raising Ellen and her older brother, Vance.

Christian Science Defined

According to the Church of Christ, Scientist Web site, "Christian Science, discovered by Mary Baker Eddy, is a universal, practical system of spiritual, prayer-based Christian healing, available and accessible to everyone." Although the church declares that all medical decisions are based on individual choice, Christian Scientists generally do not seek traditional medical care for illnesses, instead relying on their faith and spirituality to heal. In addition, Christian Scientists generally do not believe in owning many material things.

Church of Christ, Scientist, "About Christian Science," 2009. www.tfccs.com/aboutchristian science.

In *My Point . . . and I Do Have One*, DeGeneres talks about growing up a Christian Scientist:

> I was raised a Christian Scientist and was taught to believe that we could heal our bodies through prayer, that sickness was an illusion that could be defeated by the power of the spirit. Since my family were Christian Scientists, we probably saved a bundle: no aspirin, no medicine at all. I didn't take my first aspirin until I was in my teens and even now I feel a twinge of guilt when I go to the pharmacy. . . . We never had to buy any of that stuff. Also, we didn't need medical insurance. It would have been a waste of money because we never went to the hospital.[4]

On the Move

As she grew up, there were no obvious signs that DeGeneres would one day become a successful comedian. She was actually pretty quiet and never tried to be the class clown or the center of attention. She enjoyed riding her bike around the city and had a great love of animals. She once told an interviewer, "I was obsessed with animals, and I really thought I'd join the Peace Corps or go to Africa and study apes or be a veterinarian."[5]

When DeGeneres was in third grade, her family made its first move. Elliott would move the family quite a bit over the next several years. The constant changes took their toll on Ellen. In an interview, she recalled, "We just moved around within the city of New Orleans, and I'd have to go to a different school almost every year. I never really kind of adjusted or fit in, so I was just frustrated." In another interview she admitted, "When I was a kid, we moved around so much that I always wanted people to like me. It was weird being the new kid in school all the time, so I just wanted to feel like I belonged."[6]

However, in addition to never really settling into one place, being a Christian Scientist made it difficult for DeGeneres to fit in. She has memories of other students lining up for vaccinations, but she was the only one who did not have to because of her religion. Even though she was very afraid of needles and thus did not want to get a shot, she recalls crying because she wanted to be in that line with everyone else.

Her last name also made it easy for kids to tease her. "My name is DeGeneres—of course kids made fun of me. And kids didn't even know what *degenerate* meant, but their parents taught them. 'Go to school and say *degenerate*.' I'm sure they did. That's why I'm sensitive, I guess,"[7] DeGeneres once said.

Life Changes

With all the moves and struggles to fit in, the early 1970s brought more change and difficulties for DeGeneres. In 1970, after Betty's father died of a heart attack, Betty decided she no longer wanted to be a practicing Christian Scientist. She felt strongly that if her father had been given better health care, he may have survived his heart attack. She also found that the religion offered her no comfort as she grieved for her father. For a few more years, however, Ellen and Vance continued to be practicing Christian Scientists, going to church with their father.

Once Betty made the decision to leave the Christian Scientist faith, she and Elliott lost one of the strongest bonds that had held them together. So, in 1972, she made another decision that would greatly affect Ellen: Betty planned to leave Elliott. For years she had not been happy in her marriage, and now she felt it had reached the breaking point. Walking with young Ellen one day, Betty spotted a "for rent" sign outside an apartment complex. She shared her plan with her daughter. In *Love, Ellen,* Betty talks about that moment:

> El was the one who saw through it. I think she knew before I did that her parents' marriage was ending. . . . Young as she was, she was well aware of my feeling of desperation. "This will be fun," El said in an instinctive effort to cheer me up, and then went on to describe all the adventures Vance, she, and I would have as a bachelor and bachelorettes. Not to mention that it would be a nice change for her pet snake.[8]

Supporting Betty through the divorce would be just the first of many occasions in which Ellen would use her good nature, wit, and humor to help cheer up her mother. Betty believes these early attempts planted the seed that would eventually bloom into a career as a stand-up comic. In an interview, Ellen reflected on that time:

> The divorce helped me realize how important humor was. My mother was going through some really hard times. It's a hard adjustment to be a single mom and to go through everything she was. . . . I could see when she was really getting down, so I would start to make fun of her dancing. Then she'd start to laugh and I'd make fun of her laughing. And she'd laugh so hard she'd start to cry and then I'd make fun of that. So I would totally bring her from where I'd seen her start going into depression to all the way out of it. To be able, as a child, to make your mother who you look up to change her mood from depression to one of so much happiness is a very powerful thing. As a thirteen-year-old kid, to realize that you can manipulate somebody and make them happy is a really powerful thing. And my mother was someone I idolized. She's my mother, yet I'm

changing her. To know that I could make my mom feel good started pushing me toward comedy.[9]

More Moves

After Betty and Elliott separated, Betty, Vance, and Ellen moved in to a small two-bedroom apartment in Lake Vista, another area of New Orleans. Vance had one bedroom, and Ellen and Betty shared the other. Elliott got a small apartment near them so that he could visit his children frequently. In keeping with the pattern of Ellen's childhood, more moves followed. Betty, Vance, and Ellen soon moved to a townhouse in Metairie and then another apartment a short while later. Vance, now well into his teens, played in a band, and his group started to tour. That left Ellen and Betty alone together—a lot. While the two were already very close, their bond grew even deeper. They talked a lot. They talked about the boys Ellen had her eye on—usually out-of-reach rock stars. They went clothes shopping and ate out. As they shared their favorite cheesecake, Ellen would entertain her mother with quirky observations about everyday life and situations. Ellen was also very thoughtful to her mother, making sure her coworkers recognized her on her birthday and giving her personalized gifts such as an autographed photo of herself.

After her mother remarried, Ellen moved with her mother and stepfather to Texas. She enrolled in Atlanta High School, graduating in 1976.

With their last move, Ellen did not have to switch high schools again. Even so, she still had trouble fitting in among her peers. Her Christian Scientist faith continued to make her feel like an outsider. In *My Point . . . and I Do Have One,* she writes:

> Because I was raised Christian Scientist, I was excused from all my high school science classes; I wasn't supposed to learn about the human body. The plus side was I never had to dissect a frog. The negative side . . . was that for the longest time I didn't know anything about the human body at all. When my stomach hurt, I said I had a stomachcake —I didn't know it was a stomachache. While that sort of mistake is cute in a four-year-old, in a teenager it raises a few eyebrows.[10]

Ellen stood out in another way, too. While most girls her age were beginning to wear makeup and dresses, Ellen had no interest in such things. "I wasn't raised to think about makeup," she later quipped. "No one taught me. I was raised by the wolves. All male wolves. They didn't wear makeup, although one did wear deodorant, so I learned about that."[11]

Later, DeGeneres would speak about those less-than-happy high school days: "Back then in New Orleans I didn't have any hangouts; I moved around too much for that. I had a lot of different friends, but all the time I was trying to find myself. I didn't know who I really wanted to be—or what I wanted to be."[12]

It was about that time that Ellen decided to assert herself as an individual in an attempt to find out just who she was. Her first step was to stop being a Christian Scientist. She also started hanging out with an older, questionable crowd. She and her mother were living in an area of Metairie that had a lot of night-clubs. It was not necessarily the best neighborhood in which to raise a family. Ellen and some friends she had met at high school were somehow getting into one of the nightclubs; Ellen was far too young for that. Ellen also told Betty that one of her friends who was working at the mall was stealing jewelry. All of this worried Betty. She did not want to see her daughter go down the wrong path.

A New Man in Their Lives

Although Betty left Elliott in 1972, their divorce was not final until January 1974. And after two years of being without a man in her life, she was ready to be in a relationship again. The apartment complex where they lived had a pool, and that is where Betty spied a man with whom she became serious, and they eventually married. In her book, *Love, Ellen,* Betty refers to this man only by the initial B, because of events that would later take place.

B was divorced and had three children. Betty thought he was a strong father figure and might offer Ellen some discipline, which Betty felt her daughter needed. He was a salesman and had sold Betty on his good looks, take-charge attitude, and know-how about cars, gardening, and home repair.

A Major Move

Soon after Betty married B, they decided to move to the small town of Atlanta, Texas, with a population of just six thousand. Betty thought the move would be good for them. Although Ellen would move with them, Vance decided to stay in New Orleans and live with Elliott. Not wanting to take Ellen out of school in the middle of the year, however, they decided she would join them in June. In the meantime, Ellen would also live with her father. Ellen was not happy about the move—she knew what it meant: She would have to start all over yet again.

When June arrived, Ellen moved to Texas and had to adjust to the slower pace of life in a small town. According to Betty, Ellen quickly made friends and joined the high school tennis team, but she did not participate in many of the activities other teenagers were doing at the time. In an interview in 1993, Ellen reflected on the move and life in small-town Texas:

> I was hanging out with people who were older, staying out late, and I think that was one of the reasons my mother thought it would be good to move to Atlanta, Texas. . . . We lived in a dry county, which meant that teenagers would drive 45 miles for beer. And when you got there you didn't want to get just a six-pack, since you'd driven all

Ellen's Older Brother, Vance

Ellen's brother, Vance DeGeneres, tried comedy before Ellen did. In fact, Ellen was often referred to as "Vance's sister." In 1977 he and two friends came up with an idea for a short movie about a simple clay figure named Mr. Bill who always had very bad luck—he often ended up flattened like a pancake. They filmed the movie, *Home Movie: The Mr. Bill Show*, and submitted it to *Saturday Night Live*, which quickly accepted it. Vance had a part in the movie; he was Mr. Hands, the archenemy of Mr. Bill. After the first episode of the *Mr. Bill Show* aired, audiences loved it, so more episodes were ordered.

Unfortunately, Vance had some bad luck of his own and had a falling out with his partners. They went to court, with Vance trying to get a portion of the rights to Mr. Bill along with some of the profits. They settled out of court for an undisclosed amount.

Vance then made a career of music. He had played in bands since junior high school, and in the early 1980s he played the bass and wrote songs for the punk rock band The Cold. In the mid-1980s, Vance cofounded a band called House of Schock, but it did not last very long. In 1998 he joined the band Cow-

boy Mouth and stayed with it until 2007, when he left to pursue television projects. Today Vance lives near his sister and mother in California and co-runs Carousel Productions, actor and comedian Steve Carrell's production company.

Ellen and her brother, Vance, attend the fifty-second annual Golden Globe Awards in 1995.

that far, so you got a case. So we'd go out in the middle of a big field and build a bonfire and drink beer. At that time, the height of aspirations was to get your name in iridescent letters on the back of your boyfriend's pickup truck. You can see why the day after graduation from high school, I headed back to New Orleans.[13]

But again Ellen used her humor to fit in and make new friends in Texas. Later she would say, "Instead of being the pretty girl people flocked to, I was the one who said something to make them pay attention."[14] Yet again it was not easy for Ellen to fit in. For one thing, she was a bit on the heavy side. Before her move to Texas, she had put on weight, consoling herself with food since learning about having to move. What is more, she was feeling homesick for New Orleans and suffered bouts of depression. Being Ellen, though, she put on a good face, doing her best to smile and be cheerful. Classmates and teachers from her high school remember her as being a good student with a good sense of humor.

Ellen also went on dates with boys and even had steady boyfriends throughout high school. One actually put her name on his pickup truck! During her senior year, she became serious with a boy named Ben. He gave her a promise ring, and for a while she was convinced she wanted to marry him. But Ben had plans to go away to college, and they knew they needed to put their relationship on hold and wait to get married. It was soon after that relationship ended that Ellen started to feel she was actually attracted to women. But these feelings confused her, and she tried to ignore them.

Betty's Breast Cancer

In 1975 Ellen and Betty's relationship would continue to grow. After Betty discovered a lump in her right breast, she made an appointment for a biopsy, a medical procedure, to have it studied. Ellen wanted to go to the hospital with her mother that day, but Betty convinced her it was not necessary.

While performing the biopsy, the doctors found that the lump was malignant, or cancerous, so they removed her entire breast—

Betty and Ellen's relationship would grow even stronger when Betty was diagnosed with breast cancer in 1975.

without Betty's knowledge. While she was under anesthesia, B had given the doctors permission to do the procedure. For the next two days in the hospital, Ellen was constantly at her mother's side. As Betty recalls, "B was in and out, but El hardly left my side. We had seen each other through a lot of loss already. But this was different. We had no experience whatsoever with illness. . . . To see me lying in that bed, dejected and shocked, must have been terrifying for Ellen. And yet she remained strong and calm, attending to my every need."[15]

In an interview with *USA Today* in 2007, Betty and Ellen talked about helping each other through this hard time: "Everything was a little dirty secret back then," Ellen said. "The fact that she [Betty] had a mastectomy was not spoken of. She tried to shield me from it a little bit, but she needed my help with recovery and physical rehabilitation. It bonded us even more." Betty chimed in, "It's a very special relationship that I do not take for granted. We've been there for each other."[16]

Moving On

With high school graduation fast approaching, Ellen had no idea what she wanted to do next. She really did not like school and had no desire to go to college. She enjoyed playing tennis but was not good enough to play professionally. She also played golf and sang, but she doubted she could make a career of either one. She also knew she did not want to work as a secretary or in a factory.

B was not happy with Ellen's lack of goals and motivation. He tried to help her by making suggestions, but Ellen rejected all of them. One time, he yelled at Ellen for how she was cleaning the toilet. She started to cry, and Betty came to her rescue. Betty recalls, "I could see the conflict in her face. On the one hand, she was furious with the man I had chosen to be my husband; on the other hand, she loved me and wanted me to be happy with him."[17] During this time Ellen often stayed away from home just to avoid B. It would not be until many years later that she would reveal to her mother exactly why she did not want to be around him.

Although Ellen was not sure what she wanted to do with her life, one thing was certain: She did not want to stay in Atlanta,

A Classic Ellen DeGeneres Quote

"In the beginning there was nothing. God said, 'Let there be light!' And there was light. There was still nothing, but you could see it a whole lot better."

Quoted in Quotations Page, "Quotations by Author: Ellen DeGeneres." www.quotations page.com/quote/32618.html.

Texas. Small-town life was not for her. So she made plans to move back to Louisiana and live with her father and his new wife until she could afford a place of her own. She would leave the day after graduation. Betty was heartsick, but she knew she could not stop her daughter.

In June 1976, when moving day arrived, Ellen DeGeneres packed up her yellow Volkswagen and hugged her mother good-bye.

Chapter 2

Finding Ellen

E llen DeGeneres could not get out of Atlanta, Texas, fast enough. Yet although she was relieved to leave B and small-town life behind her, it was heart wrenching to leave her mother. The two had been through so much together and had grown very close. They had never been apart for more than a couple of months. But again, DeGeneres's humor would get them through some hard times.

Home Again

Happy to be back in New Orleans, but with no job, DeGeneres decided to give college a try. She enrolled as a communications student at the University of New Orleans. She admitted that she hated school, but she went to college because it is what everyone else her age was doing. But she remembers sitting in lectures and thinking that whatever the subject matter was—the history of Greek theater, for example—it was not what she wanted to know about.

DeGeneres was a college student for just one semester. She then spent her time looking for work—and she found it, again and again. She held some jobs for weeks or months; others lasted only a few hours. How long she lasted depended on how bored or restless she became. She held a good variety of jobs: She was an employment counselor, babysat children, worked at a car wash, wrapped packages in a department store, did accounting for a wig store, worked at a chain clothing store, shucked oysters,

"Boy, Did That Job Suck"

DeGeneres's stint as a vacuum cleaner salesperson would be the inspiration for one of the first jokes she used in her stand-up routine. She would say, "I'd go to different stores and demonstrate when people were shopping. I'd throw mud in front of them. That's what I did. Boy, did that job suck."

DeGeneres also found humor to be a useful selling tool. She admits she was good at coming up with something funny to help connect with people and make a sale. She recounts a story in which the most expensive vacuum cleaner had a light on the front of it. She was trying to sell one to a woman who asked her why she would need a light on the front of her vac-

uum cleaner. DeGeneres quipped, "That's so you can vacuum at night and not wake people up by turning on the lights." The woman bought the vacuum cleaner.

Quoted in Kathleen Tracy, *Ellen: The Real Story of Ellen DeGeneres*. Secaucus, NJ: Carol, 1999, p. 29.

Ellen used her experiences from working at various menial jobs as the basis for some of her earlier stand-up routines.

worked as a landscaper, painted houses, waited tables, and even sold vacuum cleaners.

When DeGeneres was not working, she hung out with friends. And she realized that she was attracted to women. It was during this time that she came to terms with the fact that she was indeed gay. Because she was in New Orleans—a big, liberal city—she was able to find a group of people among whom she felt comfortable, who allowed her to be herself. She went to gay bars, started to date women, and even fell in love with a woman named Kat.

Back and Forth

Although DeGeneres had friends and felt at home in New Orleans, she struggled with what to do with herself. She realized she had been in New Orleans for three years and had yet to find a calling that she felt passionate about, that she wanted to do the rest of her life. She also realized that something important was missing in her life: her mother. In keeping with her childhood pattern of constant moves, DeGeneres would move back and forth between Atlanta, Texas, and New Orleans on three different occasions. She did not want to be back in small-town America, but she wanted to be with her mother. Betty was the one person Ellen felt could help motivate her, to help her find her way in life.

Betty was always happy to see Ellen. Being apart was hard on both of them. Ellen needed time to figure out what she was going to do with her life, and Betty was more than happy to give her that time. But B was not happy with the situation. He could not understand why Betty was so patient with her daughter. He felt Ellen should have been working. Betty did not have to defend her daughter for long, however, because the small size of the town usually drove Ellen crazy, and within weeks she was back in New Orleans.

During this time, DeGeneres started to do some writing. She wrote humor pieces that she thought she might submit to magazines such as *Ms.* and *National Lampoon*. She never did submit them, however. Instead, she stored them away while she struggled to find her calling.

"Mom, I'm Gay"

Back in New Orleans, DeGeneres eventually moved in with Kat. According to those around them, the two were friends and then fell deeply in love. Kat was a poet, and DeGeneres thought the two would be together forever. Encouraged by her girlfriend, DeGeneres continued to write. She never sent anything out to magazines, but she shared her work with Kat and Betty.

A few months after DeGeneres made her last move back to New Orleans, she decided it was time to be honest about her sexuality with the one person who meant the most to her—her mother. In 1978, while twenty-year-old Ellen and her mother were on a trip to Pass Christian, Mississippi, to visit Betty's sister and her family, Ellen and Betty took a stroll along the beach.

Ellen confessed to Betty that she had fallen in love. Betty was thrilled for her daughter and told her so. But then Ellen revealed the whole truth: "Mom, I'm gay."[18] She was in love with a woman. In her book, *Love, Ellen*, Betty recalls:

> As she cried and I hugged her, a hailstorm of conflicting emotions continued to pummel me from every direction. There was my shock and disbelief, yes, together with my fear. . . . As it must be for all mothers, the prospect of either one of my kids being hurt was unbearable. And with this revelation from Ellen, I was probably even more scared, mainly because of my ignorance. How could I protect her from the unknown?
>
> Since I couldn't, my irrational impulse was somehow to convince her that this wasn't really who she was. And so, when I asked, "Maybe this is just a phase?" Ellen took it to mean that I was ashamed of her.[19]

Although Betty was shocked, she always knew she would love her daughter no matter what. After all, this is what she had taught both of her children. She was not ashamed of Ellen, but she admits she knew nothing about homosexuality, and she wanted to understand her daughter and what she would be going through. So Betty quickly learned what she could about homosexuality, reading books and articles about the topic.

Were There Early Clues?

*A*ccording to Betty DeGeneres in her 1999 book, Love, Ellen: A Mother/Daughter Journey, *years after Ellen came out to her, Ellen would kid Betty about not being aware of clues to her sexuality while growing up:*

> Many years later, a good while after she came out to me as a lesbian, Ellen still couldn't understand that I'd had no inkling beforehand. She would point to pictures of herself in ties and short pixie haircuts, saying, tongue in cheek, "No, of course not, there were no clues."
>
> I do recall one funny incident of confusion when El was about six and we went for a weekend to Gulfport, Mississippi. We stayed at the very nice Edgewater Hotel—a stay which I had won for us in some sort of Hammond organ contest. El had short straight hair and bangs at that time. Though she did wear dresses, while on vacation she mostly wore shorts and T-shirts. One morning while Elliott was in the elevator with Vance and Ellen, a hotel guest asked, "Is that a little boy or a little girl?"
>
> In a huff, Elliott replied, "That's a little girl." Then, as the elevator reached its destination, without missing a beat, he turned to Ellen and said, "Come on Albert," as they got out. Just more of her dad's instant humor.

Betty DeGeneres, *Love, Ellen: A Mother/Daughter Journey.* New York: Rob Weisbach, 1999, p. 71.

In a 2004 interview with Stone Phillips on *Dateline NBC*, Ellen DeGeneres talked about telling her mother the truth:

First of all, she didn't understand it, and then she went to the library and read about homosexuality, which I can only imagine what those books were. You know? She probably first got *Homo sapiens* and read that. That's probably the only book they had. Well, what's wrong with that? So what, she's a Homo sapien? Aren't we all? But, see she was great.

All this—thought it was a phase. And she thought I'd, you know, go through it and—like the tube top. Oh, she won't wear that after a certain amount of time. And I don't.[20]

As Betty struggled to understand what her daughter was going through, she had many questions. *Whose fault was it? Why did it happen? Was it caused by Ellen's experiences? Who would take care of Ellen if she did not get married?* And, she wanted to know: *What about having children?* She discussed her concerns with Ellen, and at one point asked her if maybe she just had not yet met the right young man.

Later that year, when Ellen brought a man home to celebrate Christmas, Betty thought maybe Ellen might not be gay after all. But after seeing her and the man together, Betty knew "the right man wasn't going to 'save' Ellen. She didn't need saving. What a breakthrough that realization was for me!"[21] Soon Ellen felt more comfortable bringing Betty into her circle of friends. Betty writes, "El had once said that I probably would never completely understand. I'm happy to say she was wrong about that. I'm even happier that she was willing to give me time—to learn, to reason, to see. That's all I needed."[22]

Betty would eventually do much more than completely understand—she would become her daughter's greatest supporter and an advocate for the gay and lesbian community, helping other families learn to accept their homosexual sons and daughters for who they are.

Elliott's Reaction

Ellen's father, Elliott, on the other hand, did not take the news as well. At the time she told him she was gay, Ellen was living with him; his wife, Virginia; and Virginia's two daughters. When Ellen told them about her sexuality, Elliott and Virginia asked her to move out. They told her they thought she would be a bad influence on her young stepsisters.

Elliott was not going to let Ellen be homeless, however. He helped her get a loan so she could pay for an apartment. Ellen was hurt by her father's reaction, but she still loved him. Later she would tell an interviewer, "I didn't acknowledge it for years, that was bad, because they loved me and I loved them, and yet they didn't want me in the house. They didn't want *that* to be around her little girls."[23]

Later, Elliott admitted that it was not right for him to tell Ellen to leave. "I was wrong, just that simple. Was it ignorance? I don't know. I never really studied it or read about it and thought about it. I guess when you don't have all the facts in anything, that's a factor of some ignorance."[24]

A Secret from the Public

Although DeGeneres was honest with those closest to her, she did not "come out" to everyone. She would keep her sexuality a secret from the public for almost twenty more years. Many people had their suspicions, but DeGeneres and her mother did their best to put off the questions and comments. And this secret they carried between them strengthened their bond even more.

Still separated by distance, Betty wanted to hear from her children. She sent Ellen a stack of preaddressed, prestamped envelopes. She thought that way they could stay in constant contact and save money on phone calls. Ellen immediately took to it and

In 1980 Ellen performed her first stand-up routine at the Saenger Theatre in New Orleans.

wrote to her mother frequently. Betty sent some to Vance, too, but he was not good about using them.

In 1980 Ellen DeGeneres was selling season subscriptions to plays at Saenger Theatre in New Orleans. Soon she was hanging out with theater people, and the idea of doing stand-up comedy came to her. Sometime between August 4 and September 9 of that year, DeGeneres performed her first routine. Some friends asked DeGeneres to help them out with a luncheon benefit. DeGeneres recalls:

> Somebody needed to raise money for something, and no one had access to Eddie Murphy or Aerosmith, so they put a band together and asked me to go onstage and be funny. . . . I had no material; I had nothing to talk about. I couldn't think of anything funny. So I ate the whole time I was up there.
>
> I always thought it was funny when people have something to tell you and they take a huge bite of something, and then they make you wait, to finish that bite. And then when they're halfway through the sentence, they take another bite.
>
> So I got onstage and said, "I gotta tell you about the funniest thing that happened to me the other day. But I'm sorry, this is the only chance I'm going to get to sit down and eat today, so if you don't mind, I'm going to eat my lunch."[25]

DeGeneres started to tell her "story" and took a bite of a hamburger she had bought on her way to the show. Her audience, though small, loved the routine and they loved DeGeneres. Later, when she would talk about that experience, she would say she loved it and that it gave her the greatest feeling. Right after the show, someone approached DeGeneres about appearing at a coffeehouse on the campus of the University of New Orleans. She agreed right away but then felt nervous, worried that she would not have enough material. That night she looked over the material she had written years earlier for magazines but had never submitted. Suddenly she was filled with confidence. What she had written would be perfect for a stand-up routine. She added a few more stories, and she was ready.

For her stand-up routine, Ellen relies more on funny storytelling than on telling jokes.

DeGeneres received good reviews for her coffeehouse show, was mentioned in the *Times Picayune* newspaper, and received fifteen dollars to boot. She snipped the article and sent it to her mother, who was still in Texas. DeGeneres was soon asked to perform at other small venues at other colleges in the area. Betty drove to New Orleans and invited a cousin to go see Ellen perform. Elliott was also there that night. At first, Betty admits, she thought stand-up comedy was going to be just another one of her daughter's passing interests. But after just ten minutes of watching her daughter perform, Betty felt this was definitely different:

> Since I've never been a fan of jokes, I was pleased to see that Ellen didn't tell jokes; instead she told funny stories and played off real or imagined situations. Her delivery, even then, was crisp—with her deadpan, fresh-faced, girl-next-door expression, she made the absurd even more laughable. . . . After the performance, Ellen came out and sat with us, accepting a round of congratulations and praise. After all the others had their say, it was my turn. First, I gave her a big hug and told her how great she was. And then I added, "El, I'll help you in any way I can." I knew this was it. She was really on to something.[26]

A Calling, at Last

Finally feeling as though she had found her calling, Ellen took her mother up on her offer to help. In October 1980 she wrote to Betty and asked if she would buy her a cassette player. She wanted to record her routines and study them so that she could perfect her delivery. In return, Ellen said, she would one day repay her with a brand-new car and/or a condominium in Dallas. Betty was more than happy to help, and Ellen worked on her comedy with renewed enthusiasm.

By November, however, her energy started to wane. Comedy work did not come, and she was running out of money. But by December her luck would change, when Clyde's Comedy Corner opened in the French Quarter, a busy area of New Orleans. DeGeneres auditioned to work at the club, and she became one of the first stand-up comics hired by owner Clyde Ambercrombie. She was given a regular Monday night gig and was paid fifteen dollars a night. Then one night a man named Marty Bensen, a VIP in the comedy business who had caught DeGeneres's act, told her she was a natural, that she was really funny. He then predicted that she was going to make it big as a comedian.

Soon DeGeneres was asked to emcee, or act as the host, of other shows held at the club. This gave her a chance to study a variety of professional comedians, to see what they were doing and learn from their experiences. It also gave her ample opportunity to improve her own comedic skills, as she was able to practice improvisation—or making up jokes or commentary on the spot—as she introduced other acts and responded to their performances and to the audiences' reactions.

DeGeneres felt good about her future. She got busy polishing her material and writing new routines. She had come a long way, from doing odd jobs to finally—maybe—finding her true calling. Over the next several years she would work hard to make a name for herself—fueled by both comedy and tragedy.

Chapter 3

The Courage to Stand Up

By the summer of 1981, DeGeneres was doing small out-of-town shows and getting more and more excited about the prospect of a career in comedy. But just as her life was looking up, she experienced a great personal tragedy. In a 2007 interview with *W* magazine, DeGeneres described what happened:

> [Kat and I] had a fight. I left to go stay with friends to try to teach her a lesson. . . . My brother's band was performing. She went looking for me. It was really, really loud, and she was there and she kept saying, "When are you coming back home?" And I kept going, "I can't . . . I can't hear you. What?" I was being really aloof. She kept saying, "Come back home," and then she left. I left a few minutes later, and we passed an accident. The car was split in two. . . . The next morning her sister came and said, "Kat died last night." And I realized that I had passed it. So I was devastated but just trying to make sense of it. They said she was alive for three hours. Could I have saved her? And why didn't I stop? . . . I was just talking to her, and if I had said, "Yes, I'll go home with you," she wouldn't have been in that car.[27]

DeGeneres was overwhelmed by her loss, but she again used her gift of humor to help get her through the difficult period. Unable to afford the apartment she had shared with Kat, DeGeneres found herself living in a tiny, flea-ridden dump of an apartment. She found herself lying on a mattress on the floor, trying to understand what had happened, as she explained in a 1994 interview:

> I'm laying on the floor, wide awake, thinking, "Here's this beautiful girl, 23 years old, who's just gone." So I started writing what it would be like to call God and ask why fleas are here and this person is not. But my mind just kicked into what all of sudden would happen if you actually picked up the phone and called God. How it would take forever, how it would ring for a long time because . . . it's a big place. And it was like something came through me. I remember writing it nonstop, not thinking what would happen next. And when I finished, I read it and said: "I'm going to do that on Johnny Carson [the host of *The Tonight Show* at the time] one day. And he's going to love it. And he's going to invite me to sit on the couch." I knew it was more than funny. I knew it was classic. And it saved me.[28]

DeGeneres suddenly had a new sense of purpose. She decided she would continue to pursue comedy. According to a friend:

> Anyone who is close to Ellen knows what an important part of her life that relationship and friendship was—and to an extent still is. To this day she's very protective of Kat's memory. She wouldn't want any negative things said about her or for people to think badly of her. It took Ellen a long time to get over her death, and after she did, it's almost as if Ellen dedicated her success to the woman.[29]

A Difficult Confession

In 1981 Betty visited Ellen in New Orleans. She told her daughter that she and B were not getting along, but that she was going to stick it out because the last thing she wanted was another failed marriage. She told Ellen she simply did not have the strength to leave him and go it alone again.

Ellen was visibly disappointed and told Betty that she deserved better than B. Betty tried to defend her husband. And that is when Ellen shared some disturbing news about something B had done to her—on more than one occasion—when she was a teenager in Texas. He had sexually molested Ellen. The first time occurred soon after Betty's mastectomy.

Ellen and Betty kept the story to themselves for many more years. But in 2005 Ellen decided to share it with the public in an interview with *Allure* magazine:

> Being raised a Christian Scientist, I knew nothing, ironically, about the body. My mother suddenly had an operation for breast cancer. She had a mastectomy. I didn't know anything about breast cancer. I didn't know anything about anything. I was told by my mother's husband that he thinks he feels a lump in her other breast but he doesn't want to alarm her so he needs to feel mine to make sure. He kept insisting he had to see what mine felt like so he could compare. I had no idea that breasts are all different . . . I knew nothing. A few weeks later, he tried to do it again. And I kept saying, No! No! You can't keep doing this. But it escalated . . . into other things, until one night when my grandmother was dying and my mother was in New Orleans, I got home after a date . . . and he tried to break down the door to my bedroom. . . . I had to kick a window out and escape and sleep in a hospital all night long.[30]

Ellen admitted that she should have told her mother sooner, but she was trying to protect her mother instead of herself. It was bad enough that she had breast cancer, she told herself. She did not want to tell her what horrible things her husband was doing. She thought it would devastate Betty.

Betty confronted B, and he denied it. She was torn; she did not know what to do. She ended up staying with B for several more years, much to Ellen's disappointment, but Ellen forgave her and the two actually became much closer because of the honesty they shared.

Moves to San Francisco

In October 1981 DeGeneres moved to San Francisco. The comedy scene was just starting to take off there, so she thought it would be the place to jump-start her career. But she was an un-

Ellen's stand-up career took off when she got a gig at Clyde's Comedy Corner in the French Quarter of New Orleans.

known; it was not easy to find work in comedy. She worked days as a salesclerk to pay the bills. By the summer of 1982, she headed back to New Orleans. So far from home and her mother, DeGeneres was lonely and a bit scared, too.

Back in New Orleans, DeGeneres found that Clyde's—where she had first taken the stage as a comedian—had closed for good. Although she did get some gigs at other local places, she had to take a job as a gofer in a law firm to make ends meet. But DeGeneres felt frustrated working in a law firm when she knew deep down she was a comedian. So when she had saved up enough money, she announced her plan to move to San Francisco again. DeGeneres told her mother that this time she was going to do it right. She felt she was better prepared for what it would take to make it in the West Coast comedy scene.

To help raise money for the move, Ellen and her brother, Vance, put on a farewell show at the Toulouse Theater in New Orleans. Vance was the emcee, and Ellen delivered a comedy routine. The show received great reviews, with one writer mentioning that Ellen was in the running for the cable network Showtime's Funniest Person in America contest. The reviewer went so far as to predict that Ellen would win. He was right.

In *My Point . . . and I Do Have One*, DeGeneres explains how she got 1984's Funniest Person in America title, naturally including her humor and wit into the story:

> I performed stand-up comedy in New Orleans for about a year, and then the club I worked at closed down. . . . After that I was working in a law firm as a court runner. I worked there for about a year (until I was so out of breath I had to quit) and then I entered the Funniest Person in New Orleans contest.
>
> The contest was at a club before a panel of judges, and about fifteen other people competed, a lot of who had never even been on stage before. I had a 102° fever—I was really, really sick. I almost went home, but I decided to stay. I was the last person on stage, and I won.
>
> They taped the show that night, and my tape was sent to the contest for the whole state of Louisiana. I won and became the Funniest Person in Louisiana. I don't even think anyone else entered. Then my tape was sent to New York— it was put up in a fine hotel and given one hundred dollars a day spending money, which is a lot for a tape—to compete against tapes from the other forty-nine states. Well, to make a long story short . . .
>
> So, my tape, representing Louisiana, made it to the top five from all the states. Then all five tapes went to Pee Wee Her-

man, Harvey Korman, and Soupy Sales—those were the judges—two of whom, if I'm not mistaken, are now on the Supreme Court, and they all picked me as the winner. So I won the Funniest Person in America . . . based on that one 102° fever performance.[31]

As the Funniest Person in America, DeGeneres traveled the country at Showtime's expense in a van decorated with a big nose and funny glasses. She appeared in many comedy clubs along the way. When she finished the tour, she moved to San Francisco and started to land stand-up jobs around the country. In doing so she soon found out how difficult it was to live up to her new title, and she faced her fair share of less-than-welcoming audiences.

In an article for the *New York Times*, reporter Bill Carter recounts an interview he had with DeGeneres about a particularly bad nightclub experience in San Francisco:

> An "Andrew Dice Clay–type comic" had stirred the crowd into a raucous frenzy before introducing Ms. DeGeneres, whose signature comedy piece . . . [was] a subtle, poignant, brilliant bit called "a phone call to God." When she came on stage that night and dialed long distance to the heavens, the crowd got ugly.
>
> "The front row was a bunch of guys who actually stood up, turned their chairs around, and faced the other way," she says. Many excruciating minutes later, Ms. DeGeneres fled the stage, and the gleeful comic returned.
>
> "The audience was laughing at him saying over and over, 'One more time for the FUNNIEST (pause) PERSON (pause) IN AMERICA!'" Ms. DeGeneres still cringes visibly from the memory. "I was crying," she adds. "I wanted to go home and get out of the business. I thought, 'This is the worst business; it's so cruel.'"[32]

Although there were some bad nights, DeGeneres was getting plenty of jobs and was well on her way to building a career in comedy. She started to see that she was learning something from both good and bad audiences.

Ellen DeGeneres, Rated PG—Always

Since Ellen DeGeneres first started doing stand-up comedy, she has never relied on profanity or obscene subject matter to make people laugh. According to Betty DeGeneres in her book, Love, Ellen: A Mother/Daughter Journey, "The reason? 'My mother is in the audience,' she used to say, even when I wasn't. Many people in the comedy world believe you have to be 'blue' to get a laugh, but I think Ellen DeGeneres made them think twice about that."[1]

In an interview with Stone Phillips on Dateline NBC on November 8, 2004, DeGeneres talked about her "clean" humor:

> It's not like, I mean, the thing is, it's not like I don't, you know, if something drops on my hand or, you know, like I slam my finger in a car door, I'm not going to say, oh, goodness, that hurts. I'm going to curse. . . . The reason I do what I do is because I was influenced by Steve Martin, by Woody Allen, by Bob Newhart, by Carol Burnett, by Lucille Ball. I mean, if you put [an obscene word] in front of anything, an audience is going to laugh. You know? It just—it's easy. And I like a challenge.[2]

1. Betty DeGeneres, Love, Ellen: A Mother/Daughter Journey. New York: Rob Weisbach, 1999, pp.160–61.

2. Quoted in Stone Phillips, "Catching Up with Ellen DeGeneres," Dateline NBC, November 8, 2004. www.msnbc.msn.com/id/6430100/print/1/displaymode/1098.

Ellen has never used profanity or obscene subject matter to get a cheap laugh.

Without a doubt her second shot at San Francisco was much more successful than the first. "It was the hottest city there was for comedy, and it was amazing how well things worked there. I really didn't struggle at all. Things just clicked and people started paying attention to me,"[33] she once said.

Ellen DeGeneres's Big Break

DeGeneres's next move was to Los Angeles in September 1985. Although she was doing well in San Francisco and working comedy clubs across the country, she had her eye on bigger things. She wanted to work in television and motion pictures—she wanted to act. She knew Los Angeles was the place to be for that to happen.

Soon after DeGeneres moved to Los Angeles, she filmed her first HBO special, *Young Comedians Reunion*. Then, in 1986, came another, *Women of the Night*. Later that same year, Betty DeGeneres held the phone close to her ear, waiting to hear her daughter's good news. "November eighteenth, I'm doing the *Tonight Show*! This is it! Johnny Carson!"[34] Ellen announced. Back when she was grieving for Kat, when she had written her "A Phone Call to God" routine, Ellen knew she would be on Carson's show one day. After all, being on *The Tonight Show* meant a comic had hit the big time. Following a successful appearance, he or she could expect invitations to be on other shows and to appear at book shows across the country. But Ellen already had those things. What she really wanted was to have Johnny Carson call her over to his couch.

Being called over to talk with Carson was never rehearsed, and no comedian ever knew if he or she would get the privilege until the moment of truth arrived. If Carson liked what he heard, he would motion the guest to come on over. If he was not impressed, Carson would smile and clap and the show would go to commercial.

A Call to the Couch?

When the big day came, *The Tonight Show* ran long and DeGeneres was bumped. She was rescheduled for November 28, Thanksgiving

Ellen, who has always preferred pantsuits to dresses, attends the 2000 Emmy Awards wearing a tuxedo.

weekend. Betty and other family members gathered together to watch. Betty writes in *Love, Ellen* about that proud moment:

> From the moment I saw her walk out, poised, smiling, focused, I knew she could do no wrong. She got the audience laughing by talking about how mean her parents were to her when she was a kid: "Yeah I remember one day when I was walking home from kindergarten. At least they told me it was kindergarten. . . . I found out later I'd been working in a factory for two years."

Pants—an Ellen DeGeneres Trademark

ew people have ever seen Ellen DeGeneres wear a dress. From the time she was in high school, the comedian has preferred to wear pants. When she was asked to host the 1997 prime-time Emmy Awards show along with Patricia Richardson of the hit TV show Home Improvement, *she was not worried about her performance, she was worried about what she would have to wear. The Emmys are traditionally a black-tie affair, with men and women dressed in formal attire. Although no one told DeGeneres she had to wear a dress, she felt some pressure to do so for at least part of the evening.*

According to Kathleen Tracy in her 1999 book, Ellen: The Real Story of Ellen DeGeneres, *DeGeneres later talked about the pressure she felt to wear a dress to the show:*

> I hate dresses. I'm too muscular to wear a dress. I had not worn a dress since like 1980, and I wasn't going to wear it. It was so much pressure. "Are you going to wear a dress? Are you going to wear a gown?" And I didn't even think about it, because I always wear suits. That's what I feel comfortable in. Some people don't feel comfortable in pants. But then I thought I would, just to show people I could. So I thought, "Okay, I'll wear a dress when I come out and that's it." Most people would be in their trailer, petrified of what they were going to say. The most terrifying thing for me was walking across that stage in a dress. . . .
>
> I looked out into that audience, and I've never seen my dad so happy. He was so proud. I know that wearing that dress made his life complete. I haven't seen the show, but I saw a picture of myself in *USA Today.* I thought I looked big.

Quoted in Kathleen Tracy, *Ellen: The Real Story of Ellen DeGeneres.* Secaucus, NJ: Carol, 1999, pp. 133–134.

The audience roared, and they roared harder as Ellen said what a healthy, fit family she came from: "When my grandmother was sixty years old she started walking five miles a day. She's ninety-seven now and we don't know where the hell she is."

By the time El got into her Phone Call with God, she was being applauded on every line. Amazing.

Then something even more amazing happened. After she finished, to thunderous applause, the camera cut over to Johnny. He too was applauding and on his face was the most delighted expression. He raised his hand as if to give her a thumbs-up but suddenly he beckoned her over. Unheard of! Rarely were any comics asked to sit on the panel with Johnny after their first appearance. And never before

In 1986 Ellen got the break every comedian dreams about: an appearance on **The Tonight Show.**

had any comedienne been paneled by Johnny after her debut. So when the camera cut back to Ellen, she stood there with an expression that almost said, "Who me?" Realizing that he meant her, she floated over, smiling radiantly.[35]

That November 28, 1986, Ellen DeGeneres made history. She was the first and only female comedian to be invited to sit on the couch after her first appearance on *The Tonight Show.*

A Show of Her Own

After her appearance on *The Tonight Show,* DeGeneres continued to make strides in her career, appearing on television comedy specials on HBO and ABC and doing other stand-up shows around the country. The more appearances she made and the more popular she became, the more money she could demand.

By this time Ellen was not the only DeGeneres living in California. Vance, Betty, and Elliott had all moved to the Golden State. Betty had divorced B and was working as a speech pathologist. She spent a lot of time with her daughter and became one of her greatest supporters, often accompanying her as she traveled to do shows around the country and always in the audience when she performed in town.

In 1989 Ellen DeGeneres finally landed a role on a television show, getting a part as a regular on the series *Open House,* about a real estate office. She played a ditsy secretary-receptionist named Margo Van Meter. The show was canceled in the spring of 1990, but the experience whetted DeGeneres's appetite for more.

After *Open House* was canceled, DeGeneres returned to stand-up comedy. But now she was performing in theaters, not bars and clubs. People were paying money just to hear her special brand of comedy. She did not have to deal with rude hecklers anymore. In 1990 and 1992, HBO taped two of DeGeneres's performances for its *One Night Stand* comedy special, exposing the comedian to even more fans.

Another sitcom also came DeGeneres's way in 1992. This one, called *Laurie Hill,* had her cast in a small role as nurse Nancy MacIntyre. The show did not get great reviews, but many reviewers

In 1989 Ellen got the part of a ditzy secretary in the TV sit-com **Open House.**

commended DeGeneres's performance. According to *TV Guide*, DeGeneres, as Nancy MacIntyre, "provided desperately needed comic relief—and not enough of it."[36] The series was canceled after only five weeks.

Just weeks after learning about *Laurie Hill's* cancellation, DeGeneres signed a deal with ABC to star in her own series, called *These Friends of Mine*. The show would be built around DeGeneres's stand-up persona. She would play Ellen Morgan, an employee of

Ellen holds the 21st Annual People's Choice Award for Best Actress in a New Series for her show **These Friends of Mine.**

a bookstore called Buy the Book. Each episode would focus on the lives of Morgan and her friends, highlighting the humor in everyday situations. Many critics compared it to comedian Jerry Seinfeld's hit television show *Seinfeld*.

The network ordered thirteen episodes and planned to bring it on the air midseason in early 1994. In an interview with the *New York Times*, DeGeneres said, "I was laughing out loud when I read the script. I knew what I could do with it. I wanted to do a smarter, hipper version of *I Love Lucy*. . . . I wanted a show that everybody talks about the next day."[37] In an interview with the *New York Post*, DeGeneres described her television character: "I play this person who's desperate to make everyone happy. Unfortunately, when she does that she ends up putting her foot in her mouth."[38]

Good-Bye to Stand-Up

With taping of *These Friends of Mine* scheduled to begin in 1993, DeGeneres went on a "good-bye to stand-up" tour, performing for audiences around the country. When asked why she was taking a break from stand-up, DeGeneres said, "I've learned that in life, it's way too important to be happy. If you do something that you're not happy doing—no matter how much you try to fake it—that will eat you up from the inside, that'll kill you."[39]

After *These Friends of Mine* debuted, it ranked third in the ratings and received mixed reviews. When the show was renewed for the 1994 fall season, the name was changed to *Ellen*. But that was not the only change the show would have over the next few seasons. DeGeneres would indeed explore and learn a lot—about being true to herself, about being a celebrity, and about perseverance. In 1997 DeGeneres would propose a major change to *Ellen* that would affect not only the show but also her career and her personal life.

Chapter 4

Coming Out: "The Puppy Episode"

*E*llen was a hit. On the air from 1994 to 1998, the show received good ratings, and DeGeneres received Emmy nominations for her portrayal of Ellen Morgan each season. Life on the set had its ups and downs, however, with several changes over the seasons. In addition to the name change after the first season, the show changed studios and there were cast changes, some of which displeased DeGeneres. But the ratings remained high, so the show went on.

In 1996 DeGeneres decided it was time to change the show yet again. She approached her mother, Betty, with a decision she had made: She was going to "come out," to tell the public she was gay. Although today this may seem like no big deal, it was a huge deal back in the mid-1990s. Before DeGeneres came out, actors, actresses, and other celebrities simply were not as open about their homosexuality as they are today. As DeGeneres would explain later, she was afraid her fans would turn on her if they found out she was gay, that they would never watch her show again or want to see her perform. At the time, coming out meant jeopardizing a career. Many celebrities and entertainment executives feared that once the public knew a celebrity was gay, they would be unable to see past his or her sexuality and would lose interest. The celebrity's opportunities might then dry up. For that reason, many celebrities chose to keep their sexuality a secret.

DeGeneres decided she did not want to keep her sexuality a secret any longer. But she was not going to come out alone. She

Ellen and the cast of the "Ellen's First Christmas" episode of Ellen. The cast included Cloris Leachman (seated, left) and Ed Asner (as Santa Claus).

was going to have her character, Ellen Morgan, come out too. According to Betty, Ellen did not make this decision impulsively; she had been thinking about it for a long time. She told Betty that she had been in therapy and realized that hiding who she really was had given her a sense of shame. She simply did not want to live like that anymore. And the idea had possibilities. Since the beginning of *These Friends of Mine* and then *Ellen*, there had always been some thought to having Ellen Morgan be gay. The storylines had always left that door open, so it would never seem out of character for her.

Betty and Ellen discussed the pros and cons of what Ellen was proposing. Betty pointed out that her daughter might risk everything she had worked so hard to attain in her career. She worried about her privacy, although they both admitted that as a star, she no longer had a lot of privacy anyway. Ellen pointed to the many tabloid reports that speculated about her sexuality. Worried for Ellen, Betty wanted to know why she felt compelled to "rock the boat." Ellen told her that it was just something she had to do. There was no question that Ellen would have her mother's approval and support all the way.

With her mother on her side, DeGeneres next had to convince the executives at ABC and Disney, which owned the network. According to Betty:

Ellen knew that even though other TV shows had supporting characters who happened to be gay, there had never been a homosexual lead in a sitcom; she also knew having a lead character go through the process of discovering her or his sexual orientation was something never before done on television. The odds that the network and studio would go for it weren't good. But Ellen had a powerful argument for trying. Grim statistics show that gay teenagers are more at risk

How "The Puppy Episode" Got Its Name

When the executives at ABC/Disney tentatively agreed to have DeGeneres's character, Ellen Morgan, come out of the closet, they did not want the media or the public to know anything about it. After all, they wanted to see how the script evolved before they would commit entirely to the idea. That is why the episode was code-named "The Puppy Episode." How did they decide on such a silly name?

By the end of the third season of *Ellen*, the producers were becoming increasingly concerned that the show had no real focus and that Ellen Morgan did not show any real interest in the typical sitcom subject matter—relationships and dating. One of the producers suggested that because Morgan was not dating, perhaps she should get a puppy. There was actually some excitement about the idea. But according to the producers, the idea was really just evidence of how the show had lost its way, that the character had no direction, and that the writers had run of out of good story ideas.

It was soon after the puppy storyline was suggested that DeGeneres approached the network with her proposal that Ellen Morgan come out of the closet. So when the executives gave the writers the go-ahead to develop a script, but wanted to keep it a secret, the episode was nicknamed "The Puppy Episode" in reference to the "Ellen gets a puppy" storyline. The name stuck, and that groundbreaking episode in which Ellen Morgan reveals her sexuality will always be known as "The Puppy Episode."

of depression, suicide, and attempted suicide, and she felt that this was an opportunity to send a positive message to these kids—as well as to all gay people: "We're OK. We don't have to be ashamed of who we are and who we love."[40]

DeGeneres approached the studio, and there was a top secret meeting. Her eyes filled with tears as she presented her idea to the writers and producers. It was clear to all in the room just how important this was to the comedian. The response she received was not a yes or a no—it was a maybe. DeGeneres and the other writers would work on a script, but there were no promises that it would ever hit the airwaves.

While the script was in the works, no one wanted any news of the possible storyline to get into the press. So they came up with a code name for the project: "The Puppy Episode." But by September 1996, as *Ellen* was beginning its fourth season, someone leaked the story. As questions from the media rolled in, the studio simply refused to comment. In the meantime, the writers—including DeGeneres—worked diligently to finish the script.

Shooting the Show

In March 1997 a script for an hour-long episode in which Ellen Morgan would come out was given approval. By that time, though, many media outlets were already publishing headlines about DeGeneres and the episode, which was still a highly guarded secret. Some—including gay rights groups—printed favorable articles, but others were negative. DeGeneres, who always practiced good-natured humor and wanted people to like her, had a hard time with the negative press. For example, Jerry Falwell, a pastor and conservative commentator, called the comedian "Ellen Degenerate." In an article in *Time* magazine, DeGeneres responded, "Really, he called me that? . . . I've been getting that since the fourth grade. I guess I'm happy I could give him work."[41]

"The Puppy Episode" was shot over two consecutive Fridays. The shootings had a definite party atmosphere, with a host of big-name stars making guest appearances, among them Laura Dern as

Ellen Morgan's love interest, Oprah Winfrey, Demi Moore, and Billy Bob Thornton. Betty DeGeneres also made a cameo, as an extra in the closing scene at an airport. In the episode, an old male friend from college makes a pass at Ellen Morgan, who comes to realize she is attracted to the friend's female coworker, played by Dern.

Laura Dern (left), Billy Bob Thornton (second from right), and Demi Moore (far right) joined Ellen for the taping of "The Puppy Episode," her "coming out" show.

The Reaction

Plenty of controversy swirled around the episode both during shooting and after. The worst involved a telephone threat that a bomb had been planted on the set on the last day of shooting. The studio had to be cleared and bomb-sniffing dogs brought in before filming could continue, but no bomb was found. In less violent protests, an ABC affiliate in Birmingham, Alabama, refused to air the episode, and some sponsors—including Chrysler, JCPenney, and Wendy's—pulled their commercials. When hearing about DeGeneres's sexuality, Pat Robertson, a televangelist, said, "I find it hard to believe because she's so popular. She's such an attractive actress."[42] In response, De-Generes replied, "God, it's weird that somebody popular and attractive can be gay. See, things like that, I don't even have to address those people. They just speak for themselves."[43]

But the reaction to the coming-out episode was not all negative. Gay and lesbian groups applauded DeGeneres's courage, even promoting a "Come Out with Ellen" day around the airing of the episode on April 30, 1997. And in the days that followed, gay and lesbian groups around the country celebrated.

Immediately following the airing of "The Puppy Episode," *PrimeTime Live*, an ABC newsmagazine, aired an interview that DeGeneres and her mother had done with Diane Sawyer. De-Generes was open and honest about her life and said she realized she might lose both gay and straight fans:

I'm letting down the straight community that is going to worry about their kids watching me. And I'm letting down the militant gay community that says, "How dare you not be gay enough." But it doesn't mean that I need to be some poster child for anybody. The main reason I never wanted to do this was because I don't want to become political and I don't want to become some gay activist. And that's the risk here. I think I'm going to piss off everybody. I can only hope that people are as fair-minded and as open and accepting as I am.[44]

Awards for DeGeneres

Perhaps the best part—for DeGeneres and the studio—was the fact that the show received good reviews, and an estimated 42 million people watched as *Ellen* made television history. And many of those viewers stuck around to watch the *PrimeTime Live* interview. DeGeneres received other recognition as well. She was given the American Civil Liberties Union (ACLU) Bill of Rights Award and the Jack Benny Award from the University of California, Los Angeles, and she topped the year's "Most Fascinating" and "Most Influential" lists. In her acceptance speech for the ACLU Bill of Rights Award, DeGeneres said:

> I feel like I'm being honored for helping myself. I had no idea how many other lives would be affected by what I've done.
>
> I got to a place where I needed to live my life freely. I didn't want to feel ashamed of who I was anymore. Thank God, literally, thank God for allowing me to get there. Some people never do. Some people hide a little bit of who they are because it's safer in this world to hide than to be yourself. Rather than celebrate individuality, society would rather have others feel uncomfortable and stay quiet, or better yet, be invisible.
>
> How sad. I feel overwhelmed sometimes. And I feel a responsibility to continue to simply be myself. I want to continue acting, entertaining, making people laugh, making

A Woman of Many Talents

In addition to being a stand-up comic, talk-show host, and actress, Ellen DeGeneres is also a best-selling author. Her first book, *My Point . . . and I Do Have One*, came out in 1995, debuting at the number one spot on the *New York Times* best-seller list.

When the publisher first approached DeGeneres about writing a book, the hope was that she would write an auto-biography. But she was not interested in that. She wanted to write a comedy book, and that is what it became. DeGeneres followed up her first book with a second, *The Funny Thing Is . . .*, in 2003. DeGeneres showcases her subtle humor on the book's jacket: "DeGeneres takes an innovative approach to the organization of her book by utilizing a section in the beginning that includes the name of each chapter, along with a corre-sponding page number. She calls it the 'Table of Contents,' and she is confident that it will become the standard to which all books in the future will aspire."

Ellen DeGeneres, *The Funny Thing Is . . .* New York: Simon & Schuster, 2003, book jacket copy.

Ellen has become a successful writer and has published several popular books.

people feel good. And I will also dedicate my life to making it safe for all people to live their lives freely—whatever that means.[45]

Ellen holds her Emmy for Best Writing in a Comedy Series for "The Puppy Episode" of Ellen.

Months later, DeGeneres was nominated for two Emmy Awards for "The Puppy Episode": one for Outstanding Actress in a Comedy Series and the other as part of the writing team. DeGeneres lost out to Helen Hunt for the first award, but she won the second. In her acceptance speech, she said, "I accept this on behalf of all the people, and the teenagers especially, out there who think there's something wrong with them because they're gay. Don't ever let anybody make you feel ashamed of who you are."[46]

Yep, She Is Gay

Around the same time Ellen Morgan came out on television, Ellen DeGeneres officially came out too, with an appearance on the cover of *Time* magazine in April 1997 with the quip, "Yep, I'm Gay." In the interview she said:

> I always thought I could keep my personal life separate from my professional life. In every interview I ever did everyone tried to trap me into saying I was gay. And I learned every way to dodge that. Or if they just blatantly asked me, I would say I don't talk about my personal life. I mean, I really tried to figure out every way to avoid answering that question for as long as I could.
>
> For me, this has been the most freeing experience because people can't hurt me anymore. I don't have to worry about somebody saying something about me, or a reporter trying to find out information. Literally, as soon as I made this decision, I lost weight. My skin has cleared up. I don't have anything to be scared of, which I think outweighs whatever else happens in my career.[47]

Over the next several months, DeGeneres and her mother received hundreds of letters from gay men and women and their family members, thanking them for their courage and relaying their own stories of how they had been discriminated against or accepted by friends, parents, and society. Many gay men and women recounted how "The Puppy Episode" had given them the courage to come out; other letters were from parents who had changed their views toward their own gay children thanks to Betty DeGeneres's example of love and acceptance. But they had their fair share of "hate" mail as well—either directly or through the media.

In a 2004 interview with Stone Phillips on *Dateline NBC*, DeGeneres was asked about her decision to come out. She replied:

> When I made the decision to come out, everything was great. And I really naively thought nobody's going to care, you know. It's like, I'm going to just now say, by the way, I'm gay. I mean, all of my business people, all my people, were saying, don't do it, you know. . . . I couldn't listen to them. I had to listen to me. You know? It's my life. It's my heart. It's my soul. It's my journey. And it's who I am.[48]

Ellen and Anne

Now "out," Ellen found that the public's fascination with her personal life only grew, especially since she had admitted during the Diane Sawyer interview that she was in a relationship. Because she had been spotted with actress Anne Heche, speculation grew that she was DeGeneres's love interest. Most people believed Heche to be heterosexual, so the story grabbed the public's attention and ignited a media firestorm.

As it turns out, DeGeneres and Heche had met at an Oscar party on March 24, 1997. DeGeneres attended the party alone, and Heche approached her after spotting her from across the room. They fell in love. Due to the rumors surrounding their relationship, in April 1997 DeGeneres and Heche appeared on *Oprah* and admitted they were dating. They wanted to address the public's reaction. They shared with the talk-show host that they felt stigmatized by the media and the entertainment industry for their decision to come out. They thought it was negatively affecting their work lives. The two also spoke of being together forever.

After "The Puppy Episode"

Ellen was renewed for a fifth season, but it would be its last. Going forward, the show explored storylines that followed Ellen

When Ellen and Anne Heche (front) announced that they were a couple, both had concerns that Hollywood would shut them out.

Morgan as a single gay woman dating different women and sometimes forming relationships. Not every episode focused on the gay issue, however. But as time went on, DeGeneres and Disney/ABC executives were often at odds over storylines and how episodes should be rated, and some advertisers and organized groups still had trouble with the gay content of the show. Rumors swirled about problems on the set and that the show would be canceled. Even with all the negative press, however, the show was still doing well among viewers, and most critics were still giving it good reviews.

Indeed the rumors were true. *Ellen* was canceled in the spring of 1998. Later DeGeneres would admit that no one actually told her about the cancellation; she had to read about it in the newspaper. She was incredibly hurt, but she worked to end the show on a high note. The last episode was a "mockumentary," as DeGeneres referred to it, of her career and the history of television. Again the episode featured an all-star cast, including Glenn Close, Cindy Crawford, Helen Hunt, Ted Danson, Woody Harrelson, and Linda Ellerbee as the interviewer. The episode was shot over several days, and throughout the process of ending the show DeGeneres was very emotional.

For DeGeneres, things seemed to go from bad to worse. Although everything seemed to be fine between her and Heche, on August 19, 2000, the couple made a public announcement that they were ending their relationship of three and a half years. Later that same day, Heche was found talking incoherently outside a home in Fresno, California. Residents called the police, and Heche was briefly hospitalized and then released. A messy breakup followed, as Heche married a cameraman who had been with the couple on a trip to film DeGeneres's stand-up comedy. The breakup hit DeGeneres hard, as she explained to a reporter for the *Advocate,* a gay monthly newsmagazine:

It feels like your sides are cracking open. I hadn't experienced it before. I had never been left by anybody—I was always the one to leave. . . . And it feels like you cannot go on. And I would sit and literally not know where the day went. The sun would come up and the sun would go down, and I didn't notice because I was just staring at the wall. I didn't leave my house. I would go through days of crying. It felt like I would never live again. But you do.[49]

DeGeneres had hit a rough patch in her life, both personally and professionally. She believed her very public breakup with Heche had eaten away at the goodwill her fans had felt for her after she announced she was gay. In an article in *People* magazine she said, "I went through a phase, whether it was true or not, where my perception was, 'Everyone hates me now,' and it felt horrible."[50]

Throughout her life, Ellen DeGeneres has endured all kinds of adversity. But the one thing that has always gotten her through the toughest times has been her special brand of humor, her ability to make people laugh, to point out the silliness in everyday situations. Now, however, she was facing the most difficult challenges of her life. Would DeGeneres be able to muster up the courage and the will to laugh at herself and move on?

Chapter 5

The Ellen DeGeneres Show

In 1997 many wondered why, with a hit show, a best-selling book, a successful stand-up career, and millions of fans, Ellen DeGeneres would jeopardize it all by revealing her homosexuality. But this comedian has never felt the need to take the easy road. Since her childhood in Metairie, Louisiana, she has faced all kinds of challenges and has always come out on top. Although few could face such personal and professional obstacles with a sense of humor, laughter is exactly what has gotten DeGeneres—and those around her—through life's ups and downs.

Always Working

After her very public breakup with Anne Heche, DeGeneres did not hide out for long. Instead, she got back to work. In a 2005 interview with *Allure* magazine, DeGeneres reflected on her coming out and what happened after the breakup:

> Anne broke my heart into a million pieces, I've never spoken to her since she left. . . . I mean, the way I came out was such a personal search for freedom and to get rid of shame, and Anne was so fearless. My family was always such a sweet, polite family. The way I had planned to come out would not have been in people's faces so much. I would not have gone to that level, yet maybe that was important to do. When Anne left, I'd wake up in the morning, and my eyes

The Ellen Show was not a hit with audiences or reviewers, and although eighteen episodes had been recorded, only thirteen were aired. The show was canceled after one season.

would just immediately fill up with tears, and I would start convulsively crying. I'd watch the sun come up and then go down, and I'd literally be in the same place on the floor. I finally just thought, I'm not going to let this destroy me. I'm so grateful for it, finally. I think everybody needs to have their heart broken.[51]

DeGeneres decided to get back to where it all started for her—doing stand-up comedy. She wrote a routine called *The Beginning*, which was recorded for HBO and aired in 2000. The special was later nominated for two Emmy Awards.

In 2001 DeGeneres was approached with an idea to do a variety show. That idea eventually turned into another sitcom, this one about a gay woman who moves to a small town from a big city. *The Ellen Show* was not a hit with audiences or reviewers, however, and although eighteen episodes had been recorded, only thirteen were ever aired. The show was canceled after one season. In that same year, though, DeGeneres would begin what many have referred to as her second act. In an interview with Guy MacPherson of the Web site Comedy Couch, DeGeneres talks about the cancellation:

I don't think it was really given a chance. But I think it had potential. I feel like it fell kind of in the middle. It was neither/nor. It either should have been a little bit edgier and smarter or. . . . It just kind of. . . . You know, I'm never going to get the *Everybody Loves Raymond* audience. I'm not going to get the families. I think there are people that are still unfortunately still holding on to some old baggage. I think I'll get them. I think people will kind of let go of all that, and if something's funny and if something's good, they will come back eventually.[52]

Helping a Grieving Nation to Laugh Again

Soon after the terrorist attacks of September 11, 2001, DeGeneres was asked to host the prime-time Emmy Awards. She had hoped her appearance would garner some support for *The Ellen Show*. The awards show was delayed twice, however, because of the country's situation. Many people simply felt the American people were not yet ready to laugh, and what is usually a lavish celebration seemed so trivial in light of what had just happened. The entire entertainment industry was struggling with how to amuse audiences without appearing insensitive. Many thought maybe they should not even try. But perhaps they underestimated the power of DeGeneres's humor. After all, her wit had been helping her and her mother through hard times for years.

DeGeneres impressed the nation—including her colleagues in attendance and millions of television viewers—with her performance. She even received a standing ovation from her audience. Following the show, *People* magazine printed a recap: "Forget the quiet tributes and subtle protests. Stepping onstage at L.A.'s Shubert Theater on Nov. 4, Celine-garbed host Ellen DeGeneres set the forthright tone: 'What would bug the Taliban more than seeing a gay woman in a suit surrounded by Jews?'"[53] *Entertainment Weekly* described the comedian's performance as "witty, respectful, and wise."[54]

Although her sitcom did not do well, over the next year DeGeneres was appearing on television more and more as both herself and in character. She hosted *Saturday Night Live*, made a guest

The Show Must Go On

Ellen DeGeneres has pulled many stunts on her show. One of the most memorable was during the week of April 30, 2007, when the comedian hurt her back picking up one of her dogs. She was ordered to be on full bed rest. Instead of missing her show, though, DeGeneres hosted *The Ellen DeGeneres Show* from her studio while sitting up in a hospital bed situated at center stage. Her guests that week included Ryan Seacrest, Lindsay Lohan, and the doctor who had treated her in the emergency room.

appearance on an episode of the hit sitcom *Will & Grace*, and took center square on the prime-time game show *Hollywood Squares*. It seemed the public wanted to see more of DeGeneres, and soon it was to get exactly that.

A New Opportunity

In 2003 DeGeneres was offered a great opportunity: her own daytime talk show. She agreed to do it. But a talk show takes time to develop, so while *The Ellen DeGeneres Show* was in the works, DeGeneres wrote a new stand-up routine, toured the country with it, and filmed a New York performance for an HBO special called *Ellen DeGeneres: Here and Now*. Bret Fetzer of Amazon.com reviewed her performance when the show came out on DVD:

> With a loose, free-associative flow, Ellen DeGeneres glides through her 2003 HBO special, *Here and Now*. . . . Her genius is that she never seems like a genius; on the contrary, DeGeneres seems like your next-door neighbor pointing out the obvious, yet somehow an hour whizzes by in complete enjoyment. It's peerless observational humor—nothing groundbreaking or piercingly satirical, but simply fun.[55]

DeGeneres also wrote a second book of essays, *The Funny Thing Is . . .* , which, like her first book, became an instant best seller. A review of the book's audio version in *Publisher's Weekly* says:

> The laid-back, observational comedienne's stream-of-conscience musings gain additional zest from her wry and adroit delivery. Some of her funniest material is in throwaway lines, dropped with an easygoing deadpan delivery. ("My favorite exercise is walking a block and a half to the corner store to buy fudge. Then I call a cab to get back home. There's never a need to overdo anything.") Her smart and funny routines point out absurdities in everyday life. ("Batteries are packaged as though the manufacturers never want you to get to them. On the other hand, take a good look at a package of light bulbs. Thin, thin, thin cardboard that's open on both

ends.") Whether offering tips to cover social embarrassments or grousing about parallel parking ("What better way to do something you're already a little leery about doing than by doing it backwards?"), DeGeneres is a delight.[56]

Unforgettable Dory

Also in 2003, DeGeneres made a big splash when she lent her voice to the character Dory, a lovable and comically forgetful blue tang fish, in Disney/Pixar's animated movie *Finding Nemo*. The

Ellen reads for the part of Dory in Finding Nemo *with director Andrew Stanton.*

part was written with DeGeneres in mind, and both audiences and critics alike loved her in the role.

Andrew Stanton, *Finding Nemo*'s director and cowriter, explained to *Entertainment Weekly* why he wrote the part for DeGeneres: "Everybody has that friend who's funny merely for existing. That's Ellen. You're not waiting for a punch line with her. You're just waiting for her to speak so you can start laughing."[57] In 2004 DeGeneres was given the Kids' Choice Award for Favorite Voice from an Animated Movie for her performance.

Making Movies

Many people are well aware of DeGeneres's role as Dory, a fish with short-term memory loss, in the Disney/Pixar hit movie *Finding Nemo*. And she also lent her voice to one of the animals in *Doctor Doolittle* starring Eddie Murphy. But the comedian has actually appeared in a number of live-action films, most of which did not receive critical acclaim but garnered favorable reviews for her. Her wife, Portia de Rossi, also praises DeGeneres for her acting ability.

In 1996 DeGeneres starred with Bill Pullman in the movie *Mr. Wrong*, about a woman on a quest to find Mr. Right. When she thinks she has finally found him, he turns out to be all wrong, DeGeneres's character tries to break up with him, and mayhem ensues. Many reviewers panned the movie, but they had better things to say about DeGeneres's performance. The *Boston Herald* reviewer, for example, said that DeGeneres was an appealing comic heroine. DeGeneres also appeared as television producer Cynthia Topping in the Ron Howard–directed movie *Edtv* in 1999. Her other movies include *Goodbye Lover* (1998), *The Love Letter* (1999), and *Reaching Normal* (2001).

Although it has been some time since Ellen has been in a motion picture, she is set to appear in *Dog Show*, which is still in development, and as Mother Nature in an as yet untitled movie.

In an interview for CBS's *Early Show* to promote *Finding Nemo*, Laurie Hibberd asked DeGeneres if there were ever a time when all that she had going for her—a successful movie, a book, an HBO comedy special—never seemed possible. DeGeneres replied:

> Yeah . . . I'm an example that you shouldn't give up. That no matter how bleak something looks, you shouldn't give up. . . . I wasn't being called on anything, no one was hiring me, . . . the phone wasn't ringing. So I just decided, "This is crazy." . . . I hadn't done stand-up in over eight years because I had had a television show, and when that got canceled, I just thought, "I'll go back to how I started, I'll go back to the beginning." I certainly more than anybody am aware of how hard this business is. And . . . to be given another chance like this and to feel like I just kept walking, I just kept moving, or as Dory would say, "Just keep on swimming." That really is the thing you have to do no matter what. And if you're doing something from a place of truth, it can't hurt you.[58]

Talking It Up

In the fall of 2003, *The Ellen DeGeneres Show* finally hit the airwaves. In its first season, it earned good reviews and solid ratings across the country. The show was so well received, in fact, that in 2004 it was nominated for a record-setting twelve Daytime Emmy Awards—the most for any daytime talk show in its debut season. When DeGeneres learned of the nominations, she responded, "They told me, you got nominations for every single category except the song, and I instantly said, 'What's wrong with our song?'"[59] The show ended up winning three technical awards and the award for Outstanding Talk Show.

In an interview with Stone Phillips on *Dateline NBC*, DeGeneres spoke about her daytime talk show: "I'll do anything for a laugh. I love the show. I love doing it. I get so much from it. It's an amazing thing that I lost everything from being me and then I'm now just being me and it feels good on many, many levels."[60]

Awards Galore

Each year *The Ellen DeGeneres Show* garners more and more awards, and each day it boasts an audience of about 1.4 million viewers. After the fifth season, the show had earned a total of twenty-five Daytime Emmy Awards, including Outstanding Talk Show for four years in a row. In early 2009 DeGeneres celebrated her one-thousandth episode. And in May 2009, the show received two nominations for its sixth season; one gave DeGeneres the chance to defend her title as Outstanding Talk Show Host, which she won in 2008.

In addition to her numerous Daytime Emmys, DeGeneres has won two People's Choice Awards for Favorite Daytime Talk Show Host and Favorite Funny Female Star for four years in a row. She was voted Best Daytime Talk Show Host by Parade.com readers and Favorite TV Personality by the Harris Poll's annual favorite television star list, besting Oprah Winfrey and Jay Leno. DeGeneres was also included in

MSNBC's "Power Players Who Shape Your TV Habits" and was recognized as *Television Week's* Syndication Personality of the Year. She topped the list of Oxygen's "50 Funniest Women Alive," which also included comedic greats Carol Burnett and Lily Tomlin. DeGeneres has also been included in *Time* magazine's "100 Most Influential People" list. And in 2009, DeGeneres was named the most powerful gay celebrity by *Out* magazine.

As executive producer of *The Ellen DeGeneres Show*, DeGeneres won the Johnny Carson Producers of the Year Award in Variety Television from the Producers Guild in 2005 and 2006.

Christina Aguilera (left), Molly Shannon (center), and DeGeneres dance during a taping of The Ellen DeGeneres Show. *The show has won twenty-five Emmy Awards.*

What Is It About Ellen DeGeneres?

So what makes DeGeneres's show so popular? Other comedians have tried talk shows, but few have been as popular with both stars and audiences alike. For one thing, the show offers a unique mix of interviews with Hollywood stars, performances by popular and up-and-coming musical guests, silly audience-participation games, and spotlights on everyday people who have special talents or who have done amazing things. When DeGeneres sees someone with a special talent, she wants them on the show.

DeGeneres encourages a negative-free zone on her show and has created an atmosphere where everybody feels they are in the studio—even those watching from home. She even created a "Riff Raff Room," where people who stood in line but did not get tickets to that day's show can sit and still feel a part of the show. To make viewers part of the show, DeGeneres often makes phone calls and encourages everyone to send in videos and letters, which she often shares on the air.

Aside from DeGeneres's unique brand of comedy, one of the greatest trademarks of the show is the dancing. In 2004, when Stone Phillips asked why the audience dances, DeGeneres replied, "Well, it just happens because I dance. Nobody dances anymore. Unless you're, you know, like 18 through your 20s and you go to clubs, you stop going out and you stop dancing. So these people come, and they're anywhere from 16 years old to 80 years old. And they're all dancing. And it feels good."[61]

DeGeneres Gets Married

DeGeneres starting dating photographer Alexandra Hedison in 2001. In 2004, while still with Hedison, DeGeneres appeared on *Dateline NBC*. Phillips asked DeGeneres if she was surprised that in 2004 sexual orientation and gay marriage were still such hot-button issues in the United States. DeGeneres replied:

Am I surprised? No. No. You know, I wish that I wasn't seen differently. I wish that people looked at me and just saw that I was a good person with a good heart. And that wants to make people laugh. And that's who I am. I also happen to be gay. And I would love to have the same rights as everybody else. I would love, I don't care if it's called marriage, I don't care if it's called, you know, domestic partnership. I don't care what it's called. I mean, there are couples that have been together, 30 years, 40 years. And all of a sudden, they

On August 16, 2008, Ellen married actress Portia de Rossi in the backyard of their home in Beverly Hills, California.

lose their house, you know, because the taxes kill them, because it's different because they're not married. Everything is taken away just because. You know, with Sept. 11, there are a lot of people that lost their partner and didn't get the same benefits. It's not fair. And at the same time I know there are people watching right now saying, you know, it's sick it's wrong, it's this. And it's like, convince them that I'm not sick or wrong, that there's nothing wrong with me. You know, I can live my life and hope that things change, and hope that we're protected as any other couples.[62]

When the relationship with Hedison ended in late 2004, DeGeneres started to date Australian-born actress Portia de Rossi, who has starred in the television series *Arrested Development* and *Ally McBeal* and now has a new sitcom on ABC called *Better Off Ted*. The two were married on August 16, 2008, in a small ceremony at their home in California, thanks to a state supreme court ruling that legalized gay marriage in that state earlier in the year. Soon after they were married, however, gay marriage was banned once again in California with the passage of Proposition 8 during the November election.

In an interview, DeGeneres reacted to the ban, saying she was "saddened beyond belief" and that she "like millions of Americans, felt like we had taken a giant step toward equality" by electing Barack Obama as president, but with the passage of Proposition 8, "we took a giant step away." DeGeneres had donated money to help fight the ban and said she would "continue to speak out for equality for all of us."[63]

On the Horizon

Today DeGeneres is involved in so much more than her successful talk show. She is getting ready to promote her third variety show in which she hosts and features performances by some of the best talent from the worlds of comedy and music. In 2007 the show was dubbed *Ellen's Really Big Show*. In 2008, the show was called *Ellen's Even Bigger Really Big Show*, and in 2009, the show was *Ellen's Bigger, Longer, and Wider Show*.

"An Animal Lover"

*T*oday *Ellen DeGeneres and Portia de Rossi have many pets, including cats and dogs. DeGeneres even has her own brand of holistic pet care products called HALO, Purely for Pets. Her line includes all-natural dog and cat foods, supplements, treats, and grooming supplies.*

DeGeneres has always had a soft spot in her heart for animals. In her book, Love, Ellen: A Mother/Daughter Journey, *Betty DeGeneres recalls:*

> Ellen was definitely an animal lover from the time she was very little. She was forever bringing home lost or wounded animals to add to the family of pets we already had, which consisted of an assortment of cats and dogs, usually one at a time. . . . Added to these family pets were Ellen's personal pets. At various points, she had fish, mice, a horned toad, baby birds she rescued, a snake that ate live mice (but not her pet mice), and a Burmese cat which she loved although it was a bit too high-strung. . . .
>
> I'm convinced that if she hadn't eventually gone on to find her niche in comedy and acting, she would have done well in some sort of veterinarian work.

Betty DeGeneres, *Love, Ellen: A Mother/Daughter Journey.* New York: Rob Weisbach, 1999, pp. 91–92.

DeGeneres is an animal lover and animal rights advocate who has her own brand of pet products called HALO.

But DeGeneres does not limit her talent to television these days. In December 2008 she was announced as CoverGirl's newest celebrity model. The cosmetics company said in a press release, "Ellen is a quintessential CoverGirl. She is smart, confident, and natural, with a beauty and down-to-earth personality that fits perfectly with what CoverGirl represents. . . . She's a woman living her fifties with verve and a zest for life that is truly uplifting."[64] DeGeneres commented, "I'm thrilled to be a CoverGirl. I've been practicing in my bathroom mirror for years. . . . Now finally you'll be able to see it."[65]

And while she is promoting makeup inside magazines, DeGeneres also appears on many magazine covers. But the one magazine cover she worked hardest to land was that of fellow talk-show host Oprah Winfrey. After DeGeneres made a case for herself to Oprah on *The Ellen DeGeneres Show* and left telephone messages, Winfrey herself surprised DeGeneres with a phone call during a taping of her show. Winfrey had heard that DeGeneres wanted to be on the cover of *O* magazine after Michelle Obama became the first person to grace the cover after nine years of covers that featured a solo Winfrey. In March 2009 Winfrey offered to share the cover of her magazine with DeGeneres. Just how long *The Ellen DeGeneres Show* will last is anybody's guess. In an interview with Judith Newman for *Ladies' Home Journal*, she said the end may be ten years down the road. "I don't need to be on camera. I'm not a workaholic. I love to spend time with my wife, my family, my animals. We're looking for the right place to have a farm. Someplace like Massachusetts or Nantucket, with seasons. We could get an 1800s farmhouse with land and rescue animals. Then I'm done."[66]

Surprising Career Move

In August 2009 *American Idol* judge Paula Abdul, a fan favorite, left the wildly popular TV show. Of *Idol's* four judges, Abdul had been viewed as kindest in her critiques of contestants' performances. On September 10, 2009, the Fox network announced that they had asked DeGeneres to replace Abdul and that DeGeneres had accepted. It is expected that, like Abdul, the comedian will be a gentle judge.

In the media storm that followed, DeGeneres fans appeared thrilled with the development. However, critics quickly pointed out that, unlike professional singer and dancer Abdul, DeGeneres has had no such experience. Many question her ability to be an effective judge. Nonetheless, the comedian's strong appeal may well assure her success on the show.

Finally at Home

With a successful talk show, awards almost too numerous to count, two best-selling books, upcoming movie roles, and a happy marriage, Ellen DeGeneres has come a long way from the drama that surrounded her coming out in 1997.

Ellen gave the commencement speech to the 2009 Tulane University graduates on May 16, 2009.

DeGeneres and Hurricane Katrina

Ellen DeGeneres was born near New Orleans, so when Hurricane Katrina hit the area in 2005, she was personally affected by it. Her elderly aunt had to be evacuated from nearby Pass Christian, Mississippi, which is just across the river from New Orleans and where DeGeneres had revealed to her mother that she was gay many years earlier.

In a radio interview after the disaster, DeGeneres said that Pass Christian was gone, that there was not one building left. After the storm passed, the comedian wanted to do something to help the victims of the hurricane. She used her talk show as a way to encourage her viewers to help. She went to New Orleans and filmed the damage and interviewed victims. She wanted to show her audience the devastation and to encourage them to help to rebuild her hometown.

Since that time she has helped raise millions of dollars. In August 2008 former president George H.W. Bush appeared on *The Ellen DeGeneres Show* to thank her and her audience for raising more than $10 million to help with rebuilding efforts. In December 2008 actor Brad Pitt made his first-ever appearance on her show to thank her for her contribution. From New Orleans, Pitt announced to DeGeneres and her audience that they had helped raised $1.2 million for his Make It Right Foundation, which he formed to help build new, environmentally friendly homes in the Ninth Ward for families displaced by Hurricane Katrina.

New Orleans mayor C. Ray Nagin and Ellen congratulate Sharon Karriem on her opening of a Quiznos franchise made possible by The Ellen DeGeneres Show.

In 2004, while promoting *Finding Nemo,* she told Stone Phillips:

It's amazing to me that I have achieved what I've achieved. Nothing has been easy. Not one step of the way has been easy. I'm really proud that I am strong, because I didn't think I was strong. And I think when you bring up Dory, you know, there's that moment in the movie when he's saying, you know, goodbye to her. And she starts crying and says, I feel like I'm home. That's what I feel like. I feel like I am finally home with everything.[67]

A good way to sum up just who Ellen DeGeneres is and why she is such a symbol of perseverance is to read the commencement speech she gave to the class of 2009 at Tulane University in New Orleans. In speaking about what happened after she came out in 1997, she said:

The phone didn't ring for three years. I had no offers. Nobody wanted to touch me at all. Yet, I was getting letters from kids that almost committed suicide, but didn't, because of what I did. And I realized that I had a purpose. And it wasn't just about me and it wasn't about celebrity, but I felt like I was being punished . . . it was a bad time, I was angry, I was sad, and then I was offered a talk show. And the people that offered me the talk show tried to sell it. And most stations didn't want to pick it up. Most people didn't want to buy it because they thought nobody would watch me.

Really when I look back on it, I wouldn't change a thing. I mean, it was so important for me to lose everything because I found out what the most important thing is, is to be true to yourself. Ultimately, that's what's gotten me to this place. I don't live in fear, I'm free, I have no secrets. And I know I'll always be OK, because no matter what, I know who I am.

And as you grow, you'll realize the definition of success changes. . . . For me, the most important thing in your life is to live your life with integrity—and not to give into peer pressure, to try to be something that you're not—to live your life as an honest and compassionate person, to contribute in some way. . . . Follow your passion, stay true to yourself. Never follow anyone else's path, unless you're in the woods and you're lost and you see a path, and by all means you should follow that. Don't give advice, it will come back and bite you in the ass. Don't take anyone's advice. So my advice to you is to be true to yourself and everything will be fine.[68]

Chapter 1: Growing Up Ellen

1. Ellen DeGeneres, *My Point . . . and I Do Have One.* New York: Bantam, 1995, p. 3.
2. DeGeneres, *My Point,* p. 3.
3. Betty DeGeneres, *Love, Ellen: A Mother/Daughter Journey.* New York: Rob Weisbach, 1999, pp. 71–72.
4. DeGeneres, *My Point,* p. 128.
5. Quoted in Kathleen Tracy, *Ellen: The Real Story of Ellen DeGeneres.* Secaucus, NJ: Carol, 1999, p. 8
6. Quoted in Tracy, *Ellen,* p. 9.
7. Quoted in Tracy, *Ellen,* p. 10.
8. DeGeneres, *Love, Ellen,* pp. 100–102.
9. Quoted in Tracy, *Ellen,* pp. 11–12.
10. DeGeneres, *My Point,* p. 201.
11. Quoted in Tracy, *Ellen,* p. 13.
12. Quoted in Tracy, *Ellen,* p. 13.
13. Quoted in DeGeneres, *Love, Ellen,* pp. 115–116.
14. Quoted in Tracy, *Ellen,* p. 17.
15. DeGeneres, *Love, Ellen,* pp. 120–121.
16. Quoted in William Keck, "DeGeneres on a Mission: Breast Cancer Awareness," *USA Today,* September 30, 2007. www.usatoday.com/life/people/2007-09-26-ellen-degeneres_N.htm.
17. DeGeneres, *Love, Ellen,* p. 119.

Chapter 2: Finding Ellen

18. Quoted in DeGeneres, *Love, Ellen,* p. 129.
19. DeGeneres, *Love, Ellen,* p. 129.
20. Quoted in Stone Phillips, "Catching Up with Ellen DeGeneres," *Dateline NBC,* November 8, 2004. www.msnbc.msn.com/id/6430100/print/1/displaymode/1098.
21. DeGeneres, *Love, Ellen,* p. 129.
22. DeGeneres, *Love, Ellen,* p. 139.
23. Quoted in Tracy, *Ellen,* p. 32.

24. Quoted in Tracy, *Ellen*, p. 32.
25. Quoted in Tracy, *Ellen*, p. 35.
26. DeGeneres, *Love, Ellen,* p. 158.

Chapter 3: The Courage to Stand Up

27. Quoted in Bridget Foley, "Ellen: A Decade Ago Ellen De-Generes Made a Decision That Left Her Career and Her Personal Life in Ruins. Thriving Once More, She Talks About the Long Road Back and Her Date with Oscar," *W,* March 2007, p. 496.
28. Quoted in Bill Carter, "At Lunch With: Ellen DeGeneres; Dialed God (Pause). He Laughed," *New York Times,* April 13, 1994, p. C1.
29. Quoted in Tracy, *Ellen*, p. 38.
30. Quoted in Kevin Sessums, "Mother Nature," *Allure,* June 1, 2005, p. 194.
31. DeGeneres, *My Point,* pp. 29–31.
32. Carter, "At Lunch With," p. C1.
33. Quoted in Tracy, *Ellen*, p. 52.
34. Quoted in DeGeneres, *Love, Ellen,* p. 191.
35. DeGeneres, *Love, Ellen,* p. 193.
36. Quoted in Tracy, *Ellen*, p. 74.
37. Quoted in Carter, "My Lunch With," p. C1.
38. Quoted in Tracy, *Ellen*, p. 84.
39. Quoted in DeGeneres, *Love, Ellen,* p. 223.

Chapter 4: Coming Out: "The Puppy Episode"

40. DeGeneres, *Love, Ellen,* p. 242.
41. Quoted in DeGeneres, *Love, Ellen,* p. 244.
42. Quoted in Bruce Handy, "Roll Over, Ward Cleaver," *Time,* April 14, 1997. www.time.com/time/printout/0,8816,986 188,00.html.
43. Quoted in Tracy, *Ellen*, p. 209.
44. Quoted in Tracy, *Ellen*, p. 207.
45. DeGeneres, *Love, Ellen,* pp. 261–262.
46. Quoted in Tracy, *Ellen*, p. 242.
47. Quoted in Handy, "Roll Over, Ward Cleaver."
48. Quoted in Phillips, "Catching Up with Ellen DeGeneres."

49. Quoted in Melinda Lo, "The Incredible Story of Ellen De-Generes: The Rise and Fall and Rise Again of a Reluctant Lesbian Icon," AfterEllen.com, February 2004. www.afterellen.com/archive/ellen/People/ellen2.html.

50. Quoted in Notable Biographies, "Ellen DeGeneres Biography," *Encyclopedia of World Biography*. www.notablebiographies.com/news/Ca-Ge/DeGeneres-Ellen.html.

Chapter 5: *The Ellen DeGeneres Show*

51. Quoted in Sessums, "Mother Nature," p. 194.

52. Quoted in Guy McPherson, "Ellen DeGeneres," Comedy Couch, April 26, 2002. www.comedycouch.com/interviews/edegeneres.htm.

53. Quoted in *People*, "On with the Show," November 19, 2001, p. 198.

54. Quoted in Notable Biographies, "Ellen DeGeneres Biography."

55. Bret Fetzer, "Editorial Review of Ellen DeGeneres's *Here and Now* DVD." Amazon.com. www.amazon.com/Ellen-DeGeneres-Here-Casandra-Ashe/dp/B0000CDRW5/ref=sr_1_1?ie=UTF8&s=dvd& qid=1243378812&sr=8-1.

56. *Publisher's Weekly*, "Editorial Review of Ellen DeGeneres's *The Funny Thing Is . . .* ," Amazon.com, 2009. www.amazon.com/gp/product/product-description/0743247612/ref=dp_prod desc_0?ie=UTF8&n=283155&s=books.

57. Quoted in Notable Biographies, "Ellen DeGeneres Biography."

58. Quoted in *The Early Show*, "Something Is Fishy with Ellen," CBS, May 30, 2003. www.cbsnews.com/stories/2003/05/29/earlyshow/leisure/celebspot/main556102.shtml?source=search_story.

59. Quoted in Notable Biographies, "Ellen DeGeneres Biography."

60. Quoted in Phillips, "Catching Up with Ellen DeGeneres."

61. Quoted in Phillips, "Catching Up with Ellen DeGeneres."

62. Quoted in Phillips, "Catching Up with Ellen DeGeneres."

63. Quoted in *St. Petersburg (FL) Times*, "Ellen DeGeneres Upset at Prop 8," November 7, 2008, p. 2B.

64. Quoted in PR Newswire, "Ellen DeGeneres Announced as the New Face of CoverGirl and Olay Simply Ageless Foundation," video, December 11, 2008. www.prnewswire.com/mnr/cover girl/36286/.

65. Quoted in PR Newswire, "Ellen DeGeneres Announced as the New Face of CoverGirl and Olay Simply Ageless Foundation."
66. Quoted in Judith Newman, "Ellen Enchanted," *Ladies' Home Journal*, March 2009, p. 121.
67. Quoted in Phillips, "Catching Up with Ellen DeGeneres."
68. Ellen DeGeneres, "In Case You Missed My Tulane Speech, Watch It Here," *The Ellen DeGeneres Show,* June 26, 2009. http://ellen.warnerbros.com/2009/06/in_case_you_mis sed_my_tulane_s.php.

Important Dates

1958
Born on January 26 in Metairie, Louisiana, to Betty and Elliott DeGeneres.

1972
Parents separate.

1974
Moves to Atlanta, Texas, with her mother and stepfather.

1976
Graduates high school and moves back to the New Orleans area.

1978
Reveals to her mother, Betty, that she is gay.

1982
Wins Showtime's Funniest Person in America contest.

1986
Appears on *The Tonight Show* and becomes the first female comedian to be called over to talk to host Johnny Carson on her first appearance.

1989
Appears in the sitcom *Open House.*

1991
Voted best female comedy-club stand-up performer at the American Comedy Awards.

1992
Appears in the sitcom *Laurie Hill.*

1994
These Friends of Mine debuts.

1995
These Friends of Mine is renamed *Ellen.*

1995
Releases her first book of humorous essays, *My Point . . . and I Do Have One.*

1996
Stars in the movie *Mr. Wrong.*

1997
"The Puppy Episode" of *Ellen*, in which her character, Ellen Morgan, reveals she is gay, airs in April; DeGeneres appears on the cover of *Time* magazine with the tag line, "Yep, I'm Gay."

1998
Ellen is canceled.

2000
Tours the country with a new stand-up routine, which is filmed and becomes the Emmy Award–winning HBO special *The Beginning.*

2001
The Ellen Show premieres in September but is canceled after just one season. In November, DeGeneres hosts the Emmy Awards after the terrorist attacks of September 11, 2001.

2003
Launches *The Ellen DeGeneres Show;* releases her second book of humorous essays, *The Funny Thing Is . . .;* stars in the HBO special *Ellen DeGeneres: Here and Now;* lends her voice to the character Dory in the Disney/Pixar movie *Finding Nemo.*

2008
Marries Portia de Rossi on August 16.

2009
Replaces Paula Abdul as a judge on *American Idol.*

For More Information

Books

Ellen DeGeneres, *My Point . . . and I Do Have One*. New York: Bantam, 1995. This is DeGeneres's first book of humorous essays, which give readers some insight into her life and her thoughts on life.

Ellen DeGeneres, *The Funny Thing Is . . . .* New York: Simon and Schuster, 2003. DeGeneres's second book offers even more humorous essays from her creative mind.

Gail Stewart, *Great Women Comedians*. San Diego: Lucent, 2002. This book explores the careers of famous women comedians, including Gracie Allen, Whoopi Goldberg, and Ellen DeGeneres.

Web Sites

The Ellen DeGeneres Show (http://ellen.warnerbros.com/). Visit this Web site to enter contests, write an e-mail to DeGeneres, buy DeGeneres merchandise, or view segments from her popular daytime talk show.

People Celebrity Central: Ellen DeGeneres (www.people.com/people/ellen_degeneres). This page, part of the People.com Web site, explores many aspects of DeGeneres's career and talk show, with photos, facts about her life, and the latest news.

Twitter: The Ellen Show (http://twitter.com/TheEllenShow). Follow DeGeneres on Twitter. She offers observations and sometimes hides free tickets to her show.

About the Author

Katie Sharp has written many books for children. She lives in Webster Groves, Missouri, with her husband, two children, two dogs, and three cats.